A Resource
for the Local Church
and Community

BEING IN Arthur O. F. Bauer

MISSION

FRIENDSHIP PRESS • NEW YORK

Library of Congress Cataloging-in-Publication Data

Bauer, Arthur O. F., 1925–
  Being in mission.

  1. Missions—Handbooks, manuals, etc. 2. Mission of the church—Handbooks, manuals, etc. 3. Missions—Meditations. 4. Mission of the church—Meditations. I. Title.
BV2061.B38   1987   266   86-29445
ISBN 0-377-00173-2

CONTENTS

FOREWORD

Making Mission Happen has been the theme of numerous conferences and the motif of countless congregations as they sought to understand and to be faithful to the task of mission. It is never an easy undertaking—this effort to define the church and determine its chief function.

The little Friendship Press book by this name has proven to be a useful tool on the journey through meaning and action. After twelve years a new expression of this task should stimulate us afresh. *Being in Mission* seeks to provide that new resource.

The shape of *Being in Mission* is comparable to *Making Mission Happen*. It is three-fold: ideas, structures, actions. It is an error to turn immediately to the programmatic section, to be busy doing before thinking about being. Ideas mold us—and the ideas of mission confronting us in the 1980's and promised for the 1990's are as revolutionary and basic as in previous decades.

This book is a source of programs for the local church. Use it for that purpose. At the same time it offers ideas that will disturb and challenge us. Faithfulness to God's mission calls us to examine our motives, philosophy, strategy and tactics. *Being in Mission* is that kind of fundamental task, today and each day.

Appreciation goes to many who have shaped my sense of being in mission and who directly or indirectly contributed to my writing this book. Special note for the following:

- Friendship Press editor William Gentz for helpful guidance.
- John S. Kerr for contributing discussion and utilization material.
- Office colleagues Carolyn Kisely and Marian Fossum for maintaining day-to-day affairs and assisting in producing a manuscript.
- Present and former associates in the Division for World

Mission and Ecumenism for their insights and excitement in mission.

- Mission executives Earl S. Erb, David L. Vikner and Gerald E. Currens for support and encouragement.
- Program Committee on Education for Mission/Friendship Press members for companionship in the process of education for mission.
- Numerous and various missionaries and non-American nationals for showing me commitment and faith in their Lord Jesus Christ.
- The large company of pastors and laypersons at the local church and regional jurisdictional levels for their interest and enthusiasm for God's mission.
- Local churches (Ausburg, Toledo, Ohio; Bethesda-on-the-Bay, Bay Village, Ohio; Good Shepherd, Kenwood, Ohio; St. John, Summit, New Jersey) for nurture and vision in mission beyond their geographic limits.
- Danita, Nancy and Joanne for love and concern and grace reflective of God Herself.

AOFB

I. EXPLORATION

Great ideas are conveyed in great words, sometimes not easily understood or carrying meaning which is commonly accepted. For example, "Christian" is a word filled with substance—yet down through the centuries, those who claim the word have differed dramatically in definition and implication.

One of the great words in the Christian vocabulary is "mission." It carries a great deal of baggage which has long been out of date, but unfortunately is still residing in the mind of John Q. Citizen. The dynamics of the word, and the concept it represents, is a source of exciting exploration for Christians.

The journey for definition and involvement in mission is basic for every individual Christian, for a local community of believers, for confessional groupings and for the universal church itself. For definition of *being* will lead to a description of our *doing*.

This first section suggests that we should explore this topic as though it was fresh and not an inherited image from the last century. Two short essays begin the search.

BEING IN MISSION

"Being in Mission" is a phrase that seeks to break us from the past and place us in the context of the Church's nature and purpose. Mission is not a special interest, a function for the peculiar or over-zealous. Mission is not in competition with other programs, projects, ideas that inform and shape the Church. Mission is not related to the exotic, the odd, the different, the extreme.

Mission states the priority of the Church. It puts the Gospel central. Mission has the biblical roots of "As the father sent me, so I send you"; "We love because God first loved us"; "Whom shall I send, who will go? Here am I; send me", "Go into all the world", "He has chosen me to bring good news to the poor." Mission points to what the Church is, its nature: a community of believers dreaming of more believers! The purpose of that kind of Church is mission: making disciples. Being in mission describes a Christian, states the Church's agenda, establishes the style of Christian life, sets the direction for everything from building design to music selections to organizational patterns to use of financial resources.

Not so long ago we spoke of mission (both overseas and domestic) through the use of two terms: "missionaries" and "missionary societies." The terms focused on people—a happy fact for making the enterprise "personal" and meaningful. At a time when we expected the paid missionary to be a—indeed, *the*—key factor in mission work, we can understand and yet criticize the missionaries. The great names of mission history are a source of encouragement even today: Xavier, Carey, Hudson, Laubach, Livingston, Schweitzer, Mother Teresa. They inspired a notable group of nationals who fulfilled a comparable missionary role: Kagawa, D. T. Niles, K. H. Ting, Desmond Tutu.

However, a bevy of reasons assure us that the "missionary era" as known in the past is over. Missionaries cannot be "king" or "queen" today. Missionary societies, by definition and program, are not appropriate for the task ahead. Quickly let us look at two reasons for reducing emphasis on "missionary" and dropping the term "missionary society."

As recently as the mid-nineteenth century, a committed and sent missionary could go almost anywhere and be assured there was work to do, people to evangelize. The exploration period, with the colonial power of Europe, seemed to open gates and doors for the Church. The economic-industrial style and wealth of the "west" was becoming dominant and the model. While there is a huge percentage of the total human family that has not heard or comprehended the Christian gospel at the end of the twentieth century, it is an exciting reality that scarcely a single country does not have a local church or group of believing, practicing Christians! The missionaries and the missionary societies *did* their work: they planted the Church. The Holy Spirit "called, gathered, enlightened" persons into the Church.

With a world-wide Christian community now functioning and united, the missionary pattern of the past could not continue: a new style, a new motif, a new strategy was and is called for.

Another fact challenged the old missionary/missionary society method of operation. Local, indigenous, qualified, dedicated Christians are available and assuming the leadership tasks of the church. It is not the "missionary day" any longer. This is hardly surprising. The Holy Spirit did not call only "followers" to Jesus, but also leaders—men and women who were "Peters", "Pauls", and "Marthas"—aggressive and dynamic apostles. The missionaries and missionary societies established schools and seminaries, which in turn produced educated and effective leaders. The ten's of national pastors and teachers and catechists and evangelists and deacons that served the church in the early stages of mission work became the thousands, even the tens of thousands, of national workers of today. The Holy Spirit was at work! A large corps of persons are engaged in God's mission, all knowing the language and culture and tradition and history of their place of work! The missionary-trained national became the center of leadership for the church.

The overseas phenomenon was matched by a similar development in North America. Home missionaries, urban missionaries, missionaries to one group or another, fulfilled the operational hopes of numerous home mission societies interested in special, specific opportunities. The education and information explosion of the mid-twentieth century equips all church members for leadership roles—it no longer is limited to the educated clergy as it was in the 19th and early 20th century. The collegial and participatory style of church life which prevails now, reduces the professionalism, the clericalism of former times. Special societies are not needed to participate in special tasks: everyone now can see the whole and struggle to do it.

With this growth or development, the "missionary era" has become the "mission era." The call for mission, the missional dimension of the Church's life, the impulse for witness and outreach must be identified with the whole church, with every believer. "Mission" is what the Christian is about; the term "missionary" must be seen as describing the responsibility, the opportunity of each believing Christian. The Church of today takes the stance of "being in mission."

Having tried to see the exciting posture in which the Church stands at the end of the second millenium, we need to re-define the term "missionary." Changed church structures eliminate the term "missionary society," but life still demands professionals and necessary workers who can be called "missionaries." Indeed, the term ties them and the Church to mission, a desired sign and remembrance for all. Among the major challenges for professional missionaries *and* the church members, is the re-definition and understanding of the missionary in today's world and church. The dynamic and flexible nature of mission must be caught in our renewed, revised concept of missionary.

FOR REFLECTION:

1. Someone said, "The mark of a healthy congregation is its commitment to mission." How do you measure a "healthy" congregation?
2. In what ways does intentionality mark your congregation's mission stance?

WHAT IS "MISSION"?

This is a difficult and tricky question. Everyone believes they know what "mission" is, but definitions commonly relate to a subjective, even irrational, basis. "Mission" is a term that can embrace all aspects of the life of the Church, while at the same time it can be used to focus very narrowly on specific tasks or objectives.

"What is Mission?" is always a new, updating, contemporary issue. In answering the question, an individual group or congregation must struggle with basic identity and purpose. Any easy answer is undoubtedly incorrect or inadequate.

Frequently, those answering this question end up discussing the context of mission, or a strategy of mission, or a societal influence upon mission. One is easily mislead from gaining the basic definition and attitudinal thrust which "Mission" provides the individual, the congregation and the Church.

It is perhaps obvious that almost every activity of the Church can have a missional dimension, while the activity itself may not be actual mission. Example: Church music as undertaken by a choir, director of music, or other persons in a congregation, can reflect various dimensions of human interest: maintenance of historical music heritage; enhancement of congregational worship; a point of service and fellowship for church members. Music normally is seen as a worship enhancement and a point of membership service/involvement. But a music program can also have a missional, global and educational function. Utilizing music from overseas, reflective of other Christian communions or experiences, identifying with main themes of Church life and activity—these can greatly change or adjust a music program and the resulting life in a congregation.

For some, mission is everything rather than something specific. While there is a oneness and unity in the Christian faith and life, some divisions and various categorization enhances our understanding and effectiveness. A distinction between "Ministry" and "Mission" is useful for a congregational pastor/minister and the members. In defining each of these words, one would seek to underscore various aspects of the life of a Christian community—no one would want to eliminate or distort anything in congregational life.

"Ministry" usually reflects those things of nurture, service and fellowship within the Christian community itself. It is not navel-gazing or institutional maintenance, but rather the upholding of the leaders and members, the strengthening of insights, the deepening of individual and corporate religious experience. The nurturing and growth of any Christian community is an important function; to uplift the need for such activities is a desirable task for congregational leaders.

At the same time, a "Mission" aspect of the parish must be strongly underscored—the sense of "people for others" as indeed "Christ was for others" needs to be remembered. The Christian community does not exist for itself but for witness and service beyond its own membership. In the immediate neighborhood as well as thinking beyond the immediate geographical area, a congregation must reach out in love and service and witness. Mission is a recognition of Jesus' words to his disciples, "As the Father sent me, so I send you." God who so loved the world that he gave his only Son expects us to express this divine-human relationship in something more than maintaining our own organization and community. The Christian Church is always something which seeks to bring others in and to lose itself for the outsider. Ministry is important; mission is something different and equally important.

Many people say that "Mission" is something which naturally undergirds their life and that of the congregation. But mission must be intentionally undertaken, otherwise experience clearly indicates that we are overcome by a survival mentality, a maintenance program; we do not reach out beyond ourselves. Intentionality is a key characteristic of persons, groups and congregations engaged in mission.

Every congregation needs to ask itself which of its activities are "Ministry" for the membership, and which are "Mission" for the community beyond.

II. FELLOWSHIP

Each individual Christian and each local congregation is searching for the meaning of "mission" so that it can be purposeful in its life. Local congregations unite into confessional groups which provide a fellowship for a wider exploration into the meaning of mission.

This section quotes from denominational or ecumenical sources, providing ideas and perceptions for our journey into mission.

OUR MISSION TODAY: AN AFFIRMATION

The first responsibility is to enable each local church to be in mission. If mission is not happening where the congregation gathers to worship and study, it will not be long before the mission efforts elsewhere become futile and ineffective.

The second responsibility is a renewed emphasis on evangelism and church growth. The book of Acts records that where the gospel was preached the Church grew. We can recapture the vitality which lies behind Bishop Stephen Neill's remark that "the only real reason for being a Christian is the overwhelming conviction that (the gospel) is true."

The third responsibility concerns the sending and receiving of missionaries. It has been said that the Christian mission, rightly understood, is to wrap ideas in people and send them. For centuries this has been the clue to the expansion of the Christian faith.

The fourth responsibility is our ministries of justice and liberation to the poor and powerless. God is the God of the oppressed. That is the consistent message of the Scripture.

The fifth responsibility concerns the empowerment of women to full participation in every part of the life of the church. The history of mission outreach is grounded in the commitment and involvement of women. In face of despair and rejection, women have pioneered and risked much to minister to people around the world in the name of Jesus Christ.

The sixth responsibility is to work toward a truly inclusive church. We must become, in fact, what God in Christ has begun already to make us, a pluralistic people who can celebrate the diversity of God's abundant creation because of our common experience of unconditional grace.

(The above is quoted from a statement adopted by the Directors of the Board of Global Ministries, United Methodist Church, March 1980.)

WE HAVE A VISION

We have a vision of a growing company everywhere of those who acknowledge and obey Jesus Christ as Lord; Lord of every part of life, of time, money possessions and talents; Lord in every relationship; Lord of ambition, Lord of vocation.

We have a vision of Christians willing to go for Jesus, putting service before security, partnership before status; persevering, adaptable, receptive; above all, faithful.

We have a vision of Christians sharing their faith, naturally and sensitively, by word and deed, so that others will recognize Jesus and want him themselves.

We have a vision of churches alive for Jesus, touching every part of life around them; sending out missionaries to share this life in other cultures and gladly welcoming those who come to share with us.

We have a vision of churches in this country which have the most resources, the well provided-for, helping and strengthening the churches in the places where the demands are greatest, the facilities poorest and the labourers few, perhaps only a few miles away.

We have a vision of a world-wide network of small groups of Christian activists in every place, sharing, caring, giving and receiving, growing together, building the body of Christ.

We have a vision of a flow of Christians all over the world, leaving their natural surroundings for what is alien and confused, entering into new relationships, overcoming prejudices, reconciling; sharing the pain and being part of the healing; living out the Gospel.

We have a vision of justice; of the hungry fed; of the freeing of those bound by poverty, disease and sin.

We have a vision of the Kingdom of God, coming now in the

hearts of men and women, and one day throughout the earth
when Jesus shall reign.

Wanted: those who will share the vision; those who will respond; those who, by the power of the Spirit, will help to make
it ever more of a reality.

(The Church Missionary Society of Britain has prepared the above statement
of vision to guide their membership and to attract other persons to their
society. It represents a "missionary vision" for every Christian.)

MAJORITY OR MINORITY?

Are Christians in North America a majority or a minority?

The most obvious answers "depend on how you count." If the
count goes by the number of persons who claim church relationships in public opinion polls, or by the total of members
listed by churches, then there is a strong majority of Christians
in the U.S. and Canada.

But if we try to measure according to serious commitment to
or concern with the life of the church; or with the way our
personal lives receive and share God's mercy and judgment; or
by the signs of God's Kingdom of justice, peace and love which
we implant in our society, then we are surely speaking of Christians as a small minority. Our societal and individual ills indicate
clearly indeed that by no useful measure can we call our North
American society Christian.

If our individual and societal life is so far from the path of
love marked out by Christ, then how sure can we be that most
of our fellow citizens (even the nominal church members) have
really been confronted with the love of God in Christ? Where is
the priority of our obligation to share the love of God—at home
or overseas?

Whether it seems fair or not, Hindus, Buddhists, Muslims,
and persons of other traditions have asked why they should be
the objects of Christian witness by North Americans if Canadian
and United States societies exhibit so much inhumanity and de-
structiveness. How should we respond to such a challenge?

And also, North American Christians are sometimes confronted by Christians from other countries with regard to the
selfish and warring stance they perceive in our governmental and
commercial overseas activities. How, they ask, can they com-

municate the value and importance of Christian life and witness to their countrymen who are not Christian if we, who are seen as Christian, act this way toward them as a nation?

Some suggest that in every country serious Christians are a minority, and that we will be on better grounds if we see ourselves that way. Does that provide a different basis for us to relate to most Christians in Asia, who usually represent less than ten per cent of the people in their countries?

(Quotation from the *Study Guide* on *General Principles and Policies*, Division of Overseas Ministries, Christian Church (Disciples of Christ), 1982, pps. 9–10.)

THE CHURCH IN MISSION

Mission is an essential mark of the church. Everything that the church means and does today is to be expressed in the framework of God's mission.

The character of God's mission needs to be understood as a dynamic reality. As God is always acting in new ways, so the church is called to be newly transformed for its task. We must be humble about our possibility of ever fully defining the shape of mission. But we must continue to struggle to do this with contextual integrity.

Mission means the outreach activities of the church in word and deed. We need to help break the church's self-occupation. The tasks of nurture and worship have properly received strong attention. But such activities are not ends in themselves apart from the church's wider missionary outreach. To focus one-sidely upon those activities of the churches directed toward themselves would be to substitute maintenance and survival mentalities for mission, and thus distort God's fundamental purpose of calling the church to become more fully his instrument for the sake of others.

The word "mission" should focus upon the primary frontier between faith and unbelief, a boundary to be found today within all countries and communities. Missionary sending is not only a sending across geographical boundaries, but a sending within each community as well. Both reevangelization and telling the good news for the first time address the boundary between faith and unbelief. The line becomes blurred in situations in which often large numbers of baptized persons have separated themselves from active faith and participation in Christian congregations. In such situations, the ministry of reevangelization may indeed become a form of missionary outreach along with the task of primary evangelism.

Every congregation in every place is called to be in mission in its own locality. The whole of the congregation's life—its worship, preaching and fellowship—should have a missionary perspective. Local actions for mission are an important and essential expression of the common mission of the whole church.

Mission needs more forthrightly to be acknowledged as the central theme of the church's theology. Specifically, mission needs to be rediscovered as basic to all genuine theological reflection and Christian education. Disciplined theological reflection upon the Word and the tradition is required for the sake of authenticity in mission, while the integrity of our theology requires that the missionary element, with a focus upon the specific contexts of mission, be recognized as central.

Our mission above all will have a heightened concern for ministry under the sign of the cross. Such a pattern for mission was given for all times by God himself in the sending of his incarnate Son: a theology of the cross, the promise that God meets us in our sinfulness. "We are at the same time justified and sinners"—imperfect vehicles with imperfect intentions and actions. Yet God continues to work through us (I Cor. 3:5–23). We cannot save ourselves, but God in the incarnation of the servant Christ overcomes the powers of sin and death. The ministry of his church, consequently, is a ministry of justified sinners (I Cor. 1:26 ff) participating under the pattern of Christ's own ministry (Phil 2:1–11, Mark 8:34 ff).

In its obedient service the church is to live and witness as cells and outposts of God's new age, present now only in part and with all of the human failures of the church. Mission under the sign of the cross thus becomes, nevertheless, a present reality and preview of God's final transformation of the world. Two clear challenges lie before us. On the one side, we need to avoid the temptation to a form of mission which is bound to worldly marks of success. Can we shape our institutional forms and individual acts of mission to a greater degree in conformity to our servant Lord and in identification with the poor of the world? On the other side, we need to avoid the temptation to give up because of difficulty, despair or guilt. Our time is also marked by a certain failure of nerve for God's mission in some instances. Because mission remains God's gracious activity working through our failures, there remains genuine hope with the possibility for confidence (I Cor. 1:25).

(The above quotation is excerpted from a "Working Paper on Mission," approved at the Budapest Assembly of the Lutheran World Federation in 1984.)

FOR REFLECTION:

1. Which of these marks show most clearly in your congregation's mission? Which are least evident?
2. Which marks of mission do you feel your congregation needs to enrich most urgently?

TO THE ENDS OF THE EARTH

Every local Church is both mission-sending and mission-receiving, so that even as we reach out to other local churches, we open our arms to them. We need to be enriched by the many ways in which the gospel has become incarnate in other lands and cultures. We need to be nourished by the Christian vitality of the other local Churches, and we need to be evangelized by their suffering poor. Mission has become cross-cultural and intercontinental, and missionary energy flows not in one but in many directions. We are coming to see that any local Church has no choice but to reach out to others with the gospel of Christ's love for all peoples. To say "Church" is to say "mission."

The missionary task of the Church is theologically rooted in the Blessed Trinity. The very origin of the Church is from the mission of the Son and the mission of the Holy Spirit as decreed by the Father, "the fountain of love," who desires the salvation of the whole human race. It was to continue his mission in time that Christ gave the missionary mandate to "make disciples of all the nations" (Mt. 28:19), and he sent the Holy Spirit, the promised one of the Father, who gives to the Church the inner urging to share the gospel with the world.

A sense of urgency regarding our missionary task is a gift of the Holy Spirit that we must pray for and truly desire. This sense of urgency flows from the demands of being faithful disciples of Jesus, from our responsibility to share his gospel and from a concern that all of our brothers and sisters participate as fully as possible in his life and in his saving mystery.

We see this urgency in the life of Jesus, God's beloved Son, who was sent by the Father and anointed with the Holy Spirit to proclaim the good news of the Kingdom of God: "This is the time of fulfillment; the reign of God is at hand! Reform your lives and believe in the gospel!" (Mk. 1:15).

Mission is characterized, not by power and the need to dominate, but by a deep concern for the salvation of others and a profound respect for the ways in which they have already searched for and experienced God. The ground in which we are called to plant the Gospel is holy ground, for before our arrival God has already visited the people he knows and loves. It is in this ground, sown with the seeds of God's Word that a local church is born, a Church that expresses its vitality in the language of its own culture, a Church also called to be missionary beyond its own borders.

Central to the Church's missionary task today is a mission spirituality. This is true for those who are personally engaged in the mission to other peoples and nations as well as for those at home who pray, work and sacrifice for the mission of the Church.

Mission spirituality begins with the gospel, the following of Christ, and openness to the Holy Spirit. We need to hear the gospel and be continually formed by it; in listening to the Word we experience the person of Christ present to us, calling us to a new life, and giving us his Spirit, who transforms us into missionaries. Both a deep love for the gospel and an appreciation of its values are essential to sharing the gospel with others. Equally important is a loving relationship with the person of Christ and his Church. Faithfulness to Christ in communion with the Church is the cornerstone of the entire missionary edifice.

(Excerpts from the fourth draft of "To the Ends of the Earth," a pastoral statement by the bishops of the Roman Catholic Church in the United States, considered in November 1986.)

STEWARDS ON MISSION

Being stewards means being on mission. But "mission" means different things to different people.

- A high-school vocational education teacher is sent in response to a request from Japan to teach in a mission school in that country. *This is mission.*
- A pastor in the U.S.A. brings bibilical insight to bear in sermons proclaiming the gospel to church members and visitors alike. *This is mission.*
- Two sisters, home from college, volunteer as counselors in the summer camping program of their church, helping to provide Christian nurture for junior-high aged youth. *This is mission.*
- A staff member for the Office for Church in Society testifies before a Congressional hearing on foreign aid. *This is mission.*
- A homemaker, together with several other members of her church, spends half a day each week providing a hot meal for older persons from the congregation and from the community as part of her congregation's program for senior citizens. *This is mission.*
- A recent college graduate works for minimum salary for the developmentally disabled, bringing both his educational background in psychology and his Christian faith to his work. *This is mission.*
- A printer from West Germany is sent by an independent mission agency to one of the younger African nations to publish and distribute the Bible and a wide variety of interesting material for the newly literate population. *This is mission.*
- A young pastor is sent by the Church Board for World Ministries to work with Church World Service in Southeast Asia to assist in the resettlement of refugees. *This is mission.*
- An executive of the Church of North India is sent by her church to the United States to work with the churches here in a variety of workshops and mission events. *This, too, is mission.*

However defined, mission is at the very center of the church's reason for being. The following is a brief, working definition of "mission":

Mission is sharing the good news of God's love, care, and intention for humankind both through our words and through our deeds.

The word *mission* comes from the Latin word missio, which means "send." We Christians believe ourselves sent by God, both as individuals and together as the church, into the world as ambassadors and as stewards of the good news, the gospel.

In our stewardship of the gospel, mission is a central task. It is our attempt to be faithful to the gospel of Jesus Christ, whose words of life and saving power call us to:

- proclaim the Good News,
- alleviate suffering,
- overcome oppression,
- foster justice and peace,
- care for the earth,
- seek life in its wholeness for individuals and for the community.

So, we may say: the church is a mission community composed of missionary people.

Local church activities nurture the members, upbuild the congregation into an effective base for mission, and also reach outward in mission to the world. Mission is clearly the work that all of Christ's people (the laos) do, both inside and outside the local congregation, for and with the neighbor nearby to the neighbor at the ends of the earth. Indeed, mission extends even beyond these neighbors to include care of the earth itself and others of God's creatures.

No one has put the relationship between the mission of the church and the church's essential purpose more clearly and concisely than Swiss theologian Emil Brunner who, more than half-a-century ago, wrote:

"Mission work does not arise from any arrogance in the Christian Church; mission is its cause and its life. The Church exists by mission, just as a fire exists by burning. When there is no mission, there is no Church; and where there is neither Church nor mission, there is no faith."

> Emil Brunner
> *The Word and the World*

Mission is not an option for the Christian. The church can no more exist without engaging in mission than an individual Christian can exist without loving and serving the neighbor!

A missionless church, like a loveless Christian, is a contradiction in terms!

(From *Focus on Mission* by Charles W. Cooper, Jr., United Church of Christ Stewardship Council, New York, N. Y., 1985, pps. 4–6.)

FOR REFLECTION:

Write or tell some *This is mission* capsule stories about your own mission, and about the people in your congregation.

VISION FOR MISSION

The Christian church has always been a mission church. From the angel Gabriel sent by God to the virgin Mary, to the Son sent by God for the redemption of the human race, the sending or mission activity of God has had a central place in the theology and activity of the church.

Mission is Essential to the Character of the Church

The source of mission is God. All of revelation points to God's activity of calling forth and creating a people. Incorporated in that call is God's sending activity. The call to new life, to the fellowship of believers is an awakening to mission.

The call to the body of believers is not a call to disengagement from the world. There can be no such definition of the church. Those who retreat to study and to meditate on the activity of God find that they are driven out again to serve the world.

Neither are individuals called into the Christian church to retreat or to hide. The calling language recorded in the Bible is often indistinguishable from the sending language. "Come follow me, and I will make you fishers of men [and women]" (Mark 1:17). Jesus' language makes it clear that coming to faith and being sent in mission are expressions of the life of Christ.

God's redeeming activity in Christ identifies mission as the essence of the Christian church. THE VISION FOR MISSION grows out of faith in a God who has redeemed people for a purpose—to be sent-ones, those with a mission.

Luther, in his admonitions to daily remembrance of Baptism, recognized that daily participation in the death of Christ recalls us to daily participation in the ministry of Christ. We are "little

Christs." To participate in the ministry of Christ is to share that love with which God loves us. God's love neither confines nor restricts, but is a love which is turned outward. It frees and empowers. To share that love in the world is to be in mission. It is to be the church.

Every Congregation is a Mission Congregation

Every congregation has a *nurturing* character to its ministry. Worship, teaching, preaching, fellowship, and service to one another are activities whereby the members of the body of Christ are strengthened and renewed. These are not in-house activities only. They are the activities which propel the church into the world for ministry. They are the means of equipping the saints, the means which provide the substance for a VISION FOR MISSION.

There is a danger that in nurturing its members the congregation will lose its *outward mission focus*. It can become so preoccupied with its inward-directed activities that worship becomes a form instead of a force for ministry in the world, that evangelism becomes a program rather than a passion for people who have not heard the gospel, that stewardship becomes financial support in maintenance of the congregation rather than commitment to mission.

The church is not only the object of God's love, it is also God's instrument in effecting ministry to the world. The "mission" congregation intentionally honors mission as the dominant theme in all of its activities.

Every Congregation Must Claim Its Arena of Mission

A congregation that claims its arena of mission opens itself to discovering the gospel possibilities in its surroundings. Such a congregation is flexible when facing tasks to be done and is open to new paths of ministry in a rapidly changing society. The mission of the congregation has many expressions: It is inclusive, interdependent, versatile, and flexible. Its mission stance is congruent with St. Paul's admonition to "be all things to all people for the sake of the gospel."

The congregation is more than a community of believers. It is a community of believers called upon to minister to special hurts and hungers, specific pains and evils; to enhance the lives and hopes of all within its arena. The congregation with a VISION FOR MISSION discovers immense talent and resource potential when all members are caught up in the apostolic passion for mission.

Mission is Global in Scope

Jesus in Acts 1:8, empowers his disciples for mission in Jerusalem, in Judea, in Samaria, and to the ends of the earth. That picture of mission implies an ever-widening circle of mission opportunities and challenges. It defines a mission arena which is global in scope.

Our confession of "one holy catholic church" acknowledges that all believers are bound together. Gathering at the Lord's table we bear witness to the corporate nature of the church. We are, as St. Paul say, "members of one another in the body of Christ." There is no private, individual Christianity. God commissions the body of Christ, the church, to share his redemptive purposes for the world with everyone.

In our immediate communities, in the whole American context, and in the global arena all of us are linked together. All are linked in preaching the gospel, seeking justice, speaking for peace, and being faithful in the face of persecution. The members of the body of Christ are interdependent on a global scale; they have different gifts for use in one mission. Churches all over the world are bound together in Christ Jesus with a common mission.

A 1990s VISION FOR MISSION implies a higher priority for *outward facing* mission objectives. It calls for a mission overlay on all present programs and ministries, for reminders that baptismal participation in the death and resurrection of Christ provides mission perspective and power. It is a vision of partnership in mission that reduces isolationism and lifts up the call to every Christian and congregation to be those who are sent into the world. It is a vision of a renewed COMMITMENT TO MISSION in which all use their resources to be what God has called them to be—a mission church.

FOR REFLECTION:

1. How would you describe your own vision for mission? The vision of your congregation?
2. In an ideal world of ideal people, what kind of mission could you envision for yourself? For your congregation?

MISSION AND EVANGELISM: AN ECUMENICAL AFFIRMATION

The biblical promise of a new earth and a new heaven where love, peace and justice will prevail invites our actions as Christians in history. The contract of that vision with the reality of today reveals the monstrosity of human sin, the evil unleashed by the rejection of God's liberating will for humankind. Sin, alienating persons from God, neighbor and nature, is found both in individual and corporate forms, both in slavery of the human will and in social, political and economic structures of domination and dependence.

The Church is sent into the world to call people and nations to repentance, to announce forgiveness of sin and a new beginning in relations with God and with neighbors through Jesus Christ. This evangelistic calling has a new urgency today.

In a world where the number of people who have no opportunity to know the story of Jesus is growing steadily, *how necessary it is to multiply the witnessing vocation of the church!*

In a world where the majority of those who do not know Jesus are the poor of the earth, those to whom he promised the kingdom of God, *how essential it is to share with them the Good News of that kingdom!*

In a world where people are struggling for justice, freedom and liberation, often without the realization of their hopes, *how important it is to announce that God's kingdom is promised to them!*

In a world where the marginalized and the drop-outs of affluent society search desperately for comfort and identity in drugs or esoteric cults, *how imperative it is to announce that he has come so that all may have life and may have it in all its fullness.*

In a world where so many find little meaning, except in the relative security of their affluence, *how necessary it is to hear once again Jesus' invitation to discipleship, service and risk!*

In a world where so many Christians are nominal in their commitment to Jesus Christ, *how necessary it is to call them again to the fervour of their first love!*

In a world where wars and rumors of war jeopardize the present and future of humankind, where an enormous part of natural resources and people are consumed in the arms race, *how crucial it is to call the peacemakers blessed, convinced that God in Christ has broken all barriers and has reconciled the world to himself.*

This ecumenical affirmation is a challenge which the churches extend to each other to announce that God reigns, and that there is hope for a future when God will "unite all things in him, things in heaven and things on earth." Jesus is "the first and the last and the Living One", who "is coming soon", who "makes all things new."

(The above quotation is from a World Council of Churches' document, adopted in July 1982 by the WCC Central Committee. The quotations come from pps. 5-6, and 50 of the Study Guide Edition published by the Division for Overseas Ministries of the National Council of Churches of Christ in the USA, May 1983.)

A STRATEGY FOR WORLD MISSION

The church must clearly show the world what it stands for, so that people can respond if they wish to. The church must make sense not only to its active members, and not only to those whom we know are seekers after the Christian faith. The church must make sense to all those who are not interested in the Christian faith, whether they be people of other faiths, the highly secularized, the atheistically-committed, or the indifferent.

I propose that the churches, internationally and locally, make a permanent effort to be a credible sign to the vision described in Isaiah 65:17-23. Here the prophet reported on God's preference for society. It is not paradise. There is death, and sweat and toil. But in God's preference for the world, four elements are basic:

Children do not die.
Old people live full lives.
Those who build houses live in them, and
Those who plant vineyards eat the fruit.

I make this proposal as a first component part of a strategy for world mission because it is biblical, easy to understand, powerful in its appeal, capable of being worked out in action in different circumstances, and capable of rallying many many churches whose unity is essential for world mission. I would like to see the churches proclaim in every neighborhood that this 4-point program of Isaiah is what we stand for. Let us communicate to the whole world, "We may not have the resources and the power to make this a universal reality for all of the world's 4.6 billion people. But this is what we are working towards, globally and in every locality where the church exists. For this is what our God is like. If this vision makes sense to you, join us and help make it a reality. If the God behind this vision makes sense to you, join us and learn more of him" Will this not speak to every human heart? In the North as well as in the South, in the West as well as in the East?

Granted that the Isaiah vision is perceived to be worthwhile and adequate, with what attitude and frame of mind should Christians involve ourselves? I think it is crucial that we do not engage in it out of a sense of power and crusade, but out of a sense of woundedness with each other and with the world. Indeed, out of a sense of being healed by Jesus who was wounded for us. This concept of "shared woundedness", or "sinned againstness", is the basis of solidarity between the Christian and the world, and between the North and South. We will be working out the Isaiah vision internationally and in our own neighborhood, not because we Christians see ourselves as different from the rest, but because we see that we are no different from the rest. Despite differing situations and contexts, Christians recognize that like the rest of the world's people and our neighbors, we too have wounds on our bodies and on our souls. In case we do not, the sufferings of other people will remind us, if we would only let them. So out of a sense of shared woundedness we get involved with the Isaiah vision.

As churches commit themselves to the Isaiah vision, serving and advocating its cause in the world in solidarity with the poor and all the people who share it, what do Christians say to our neighbors, those whom we serve and our allies? What is the Good News? I think the first two elements of my strategy for world mission—the Isaiah vision and the offer of corporate worship and prayer—add up to something that Jesus said to everyone who came near him. His message was, "Take up your cross and follow me." I believe it is our message also. In view of God's high calling and of human woundedness, this message is not primarily a call to suffering and sacrifice. It is an invitation to partnership with Jesus for a great task. It is an offer of direction, friendship and community. It is a demand for discipline. And a promise of power that with Jesus and in the company of his followers, one can be responsible for one's life and those of others. To this message, we respond with hope, repentance and joy.

I am convinced that the institutional church is the most major player in world mission. It has to be. I say this against my general complaint that in talking about the church, Christians think too much of its organized institutional manifestation. Although I cannot prove it, probably the sum total effects of all the organized Christians activities of witness—Sunday worship, evangelistic meetings, social services, medical and health programs, schools and colleges, festivals of faith, international conferences, etc. are immeasurably feeble compared with the sum total effects of daily witness borne by Christians individually and in groups in their homes, in their place of work and in their neighborhood.

Of all the organizational structures connected with the church, only the local congregation has the structures to provide 24 hours of pastoral care a day to its own members and others in the neighborhood on a long-term, self-sustaining basis. I refer to the indigenous character of the local congregation which compels it to exist contextually and its nature as a volunteer organization. Even in the poorest situations, the local congregation is capable of carrying out in a minimum way such basic witnesses as worship, Bible reading and visiting the sick, according to the means it has.

To liberate the energy from the local congregation, and the challenge of partner churches for world mission today, I believe we need to reaffirm with ringing clarity that the local congregation has the privilege and the obligation for mission both at home and abroad. With the concept of mission to six continents, the local congregation has the right to get involved in mission at home; if so, it also has the right to get involved in mission abroad. This dual right of the local congregation, indeed every local congregation whether in the North or the South, means that what is home mission to congregation A is overseas mission to congregation B, and vice-versa. That necessitates respect, partnership and solidarity between the two congregations. How this sharing can take place for the good of the spread of the Gospel, effectively, routinely and long term must determine the mission structures of the institutional church, locally, nationally and internationally.

(The above article was excerpted from the June/July 1986 World Council of Churches *Monthly Letter on Evangelism*, written by Raymond Fung.)

III. STIMULATION

We have a lot of people on the journey toward seeking meaningful definition and description of "mission"—we need to call upon them for assistance and inspiration.

This section gives brief quotations to stimulate you and your congregation as you explore mission for your life, your community, and your understanding of the church's task. The quotations come from outstanding church leaders. They appear in outstanding books or other resources, which are identified and should be sought for further exploration when their ideas excite you.

THE OPEN SECRET

"Christ is the Light of the nations." With these majestic words the Second Vatican Council began the greatest of its documents, the "Constitution on the Church." Fundamental to everything else that came forth from the council were the reaffirmation of the missionary character of the church, the recognition of the unfinished task which that implies, the confession that the church is a pilgrim people on its way to the ends of the earth and the end of time, and the acknowledgment of the need for a new openness to the world into which the church is sent.

This new readiness to acknowledge the missionary character of the church, to confess that "there is no participation in Christ without participation in his mission to the world," is not confined to the Roman Catholic Church. All the old established churches of the Western world have been brought to a new recognition that mission belongs to the very being of the church. "Mission," of course, is not a new word, but it is being used in a new way. All the churches of Western Christendom—Catholic and Protestant—have been familiar with missions. But missions were enterprises which belonged to the exterior of church life. They were carried on somewhere else—in Asia, Africa, or the South

Pacific, in the slums of the city, or among the gypsies, the vagrants, the marginal people. In many contexts a "mission church" was the second-class institution in the downtown quarter of the city, in distinction from the well-heeled institution in the affluent quarter which was just "the church." In some forms of the ecclesiastical vernacular, a "missionary diocese" was a diocese which had not yet graduated to the full status of a diocese without qualification. Theological faculties might have provided a place for "missions" as a branch of practical theology, but it had no place in the central teaching of Christian doctrine. To put it briefly, the church approved of "missions" but was not itself the mission.

In the preceding paragraph I have used past tenses. No doubt there are still large parts of Christendom where the present tense would still be applicable. However, most thoughtful Christians in the old, established Western churches can no longer use this kind of language. They recognize that, with the radical secularization of Western culture, the churches are in a missionary situation in what once was Christendom. Moreover, the struggles through which the younger churches born of Western missions have had to pass in order to graduate from "mission" to "church" have forced the older churches to recognize that this separation of church from mission is theologically indefensible. More and more Christians of the old churches have come to recognize that a church which is not "the church in mission" is no church at all. Consequently the agenda papers of church conferences are liberally sprinkled with discussions about the church's mission. For the first time in many centuries the question of the nature of the church's missionary task is a burning issue for debate within the heart of the older churches. Deeply held convictions on the subject clash with each other and—in some places at least—polarization has reached the point where anathemas are in the air. This is a new situation, and it is full of promise.

The above quotation is from *The Open Secret: Sketches for a Missionary Theology,* by Lesslie Newbigin, William B. Eerdmans, © 1978 pps. 1-3.
This book represents the major missiological statement by one of the leading thinkers of the 20th century; it deserves wide and careful study. Used by permission.

FOR REFLECTION:

How does the idea that Christendom today presents us with a missionary situation apply to your parish area?

THE CALL TO THE CHURCH

The gospel is not a set of beliefs that arise, or could arise, from empirical observation of the whole human experience. It is the announcement of a name and a fact that offer the starting point for a new and lifelong enterprise of understanding and coping with experience. It is a new starting point. To accept it means a new beginning, a radical conversion. We cannot sidestep that necessity. It has always been the case that to believe means to be turned around to face in a different direction, to be a dissenter, to go against the stream. The church needs to be very humble in acknowledging that it is itself only a learner, and it needs to pay heed to all the variety of human experience in order to learn in practice what it means that Jesus is the King and Head of the human race.

(Quoted from *Foolishness to the Greeks: The Gospel and Western Culture* by Lesslie Newbigin, William B. Eerdmans, © 1986, p. 148.) Used by permission.

SENT FREE

Two fears haunt theologians. One is the fear of being unfaithful to the demands of today's world, the fear of being irrelevant, the fear of being out of touch. In the sixties in ecumenical discussions it was often heard that the "a world must set the agenda". The church was thought of as responding to the priorities set in the world's agenda. The church is indeed sent into the world to respond to situations where human beings suffer, hope, live and die. But that does not mean that it has no mission of its own except to respond; no internal compulsion, no given convictions, no values that it must share with the world.

The other fear is that through being busy over the affairs of the world Christians might forget their essential vocation of proclaiming the gospel. It is the fear that in responding to the need to fight oppression, racism, sexism and similar evils, we might neglect our calling to "preach the word". If the proclamation of the gospel of the kingdom were possible without reference to the concrete human situations of the kingdoms in which we live, then of course our problem would be easy to solve! But the gospel happens in the encounter between the word of God and human beings living in specific situations.

While the slogan "reaching the unreached" reflects the numerical and geographical dimension of the problem, the word "unreached" does not quite explain the situation. It seems to imply that there are people who have not been reached even by God, and that, of course, belongs to a dimension of reality that is hidden from us. God alone knows where and whom the Spirit has reached and in what form. This is not to deny the tragic fact that the vast majority of the population of the world has not embraced the Christian faith and that Christians are commanded to share the gospel of Jesus Christ with everybody, because it is God's will that everybody should come to the knowledge of the truth and be saved (1 Tim. 2:4).

What are the priorities prescribed for the church in our day? Three points of concentration are generally proposed. They arise from God's particular care for the poor, God's sending of the church to proclaim the gospel to all nations, and God's promise of a new day of peace and justice. My thesis is that these are intimately inter-related aspects of one and the same call to Christian obedience in the service of the kingdom, which is basically a call to freedom.

(From "Sent Free" by Emilio Castro, World Council of Churches, Geneva, 1985, pps. 17–18, 28, 96)

FOR REFLECTION:

1. How do you understand the meaning of "a call to freedom"?
2. How would you react to this statement? "Our congregation definitely gives priority to its essential vocation of proclaiming the Gospel."

MISSION BETWEEN THE TIMES

The most important questions that should be asked with regard to the life and mission of the church today are not related to the relevance of the gospel but to its content. To be sure, there is a place for the consideration of ways in which the gospel meets man's needs in the modern world, but far more basic is the consideration of the *nature* of the gospel that could meet man's needs. The *what* of the gospel determines the *how* of its effects in practical life.

In light of contemporary pragmatism, it can hardly be expected that the primacy of theological questions should be widely recognized. The assumption is often made that we Christians *know* our message and that all we need is a better strategy and more efficient methods to communicate it. Accordingly, the effectiveness of evangelism is measured in terms of *results,* with little or any regard for faithfulness to the gospel. There are three good reasons why we should replace this approach with a new emphasis on the gospel as the basis on which evangelism must stand or fall:

1. The first condition for effective evangelism is *assurance concerning the content of the gospel.*
2. The only response that biblical evangelism can legitimately look for is *a response to the gospel.*
3. The distinctive mark of a Christian experience is that it is *an experience of the gospel.*

The truly indigenous church is the one that through death and resurrection with Christ embodies the gospel within its own culture. It adopts a way of being, thinking and acting in which its own cultural patterns are transformed and fulfilled by the gospel. In a sense, it is the cultural embodiment of Christ, the means through which Christ is formed within a given culture. The task of the church is not the extension of a Christian culture throughout the world but the incarnation of the gospel in each culture.

The contextualization of the gospel will not consist in an adaptation of an existing theology to a given culture. It will not merely be the result of an intellectual process. It will not be aided by a benevolent missionary paternalism intended to help the young church to select those cultural elements that can be regarded as positive. The contextualization of the gospel can only be a gift of grace granted by God to a church that is seeking to place the totality of life under the Lordship of Christ in its historical situation. More than a wonder of nature, the incarnation is a wonder of grace.

The expansion of Christianity in the Third World since World War II is indeed impressive. Never before in history has a religion spread so vastly and so rapidly as Christianity has in the last few decades. As a result, the church has now become a worldwide movement. And if it is true, as Emil Brunner has put it, that the church exists for mission as fire exists for burning, it follows that there is no longer any room for the traditional distinction between "sending churches" and "receiving churches." As Stephen Neill has said, "the age of missions is at an end, the age of mission has begun."

The statistics of church growth can easily be used to project a glowing picture of the church in the last quarter of the twentieth century. This has in fact been done in circles where quantitative church growth is regarded as "the chief task" of mission. For a more balanced picture, however, the numerical gains must be set over against the problems that beset the church and place the future of Christianity in some regions of the world under a question mark. From that perspective, the greatest challenge that the church faces today is the challenge to fullness in mission.

Throughout the entire New Testament it is taken for granted that the oneness of the people of God is a oneness that transcends all outward distinctions. The idea is that with the coming of Jesus Christ all barriers that divide humankind have been broken down and a new humanity is now taking shape *in* and *through* the church. God's purpose in Jesus Christ includes the oneness of the human race, and that oneness becomes visible in the church.

For the Christian, to raise questions about lifestyle is to raise questions about the kingdom of heaven. It is to ask not speculative questions but questions about what kind of life is appropriate in the New Age that has already come in Jesus Christ. And here too, it is those who know they are spiritually poor who will see the kingdom of heaven.

Every attempt to define the relationship between the Kingdom of God and the church on the one hand and between the Kingdom of God and the world on the other will be necessarily incomplete.

To speak of the Kingdom of God is to speak of God's redemptive purpose for the whole creation and of the historical vocation that the church has with regard to the purpose here and now, "between the times." It is also to speak of an eschatological reality that is both the starting point and the goal of the church. The mission of the church, therefore, can be understood only in light of the Kingdom of God.

(From "Mission Between the Times" Essays by C. Rene Padilla, William B. Eerdmans Publishing Company, Grand Rapids, MI, 1985, pps. 62–63, 108–109, 129, 142, 170–171, 186)

ANNOUNCING THE REIGN OF GOD

Evangelization is a generational task: "to incarnate the gospel in time." Every generation— inside or outside the church—has to be evangelized, that is, confronted with the good news of the kingdom in Jesus Christ. And every generation of Christians has the unique and nontransferable responsibility of sharing the good news with its own generation. This is the real meaning of John R. Mott's well-known slogan, "the evangelization of the world in this generation."

There are signs of crisis in evangelization today. For instance, there is a crisis in *credibility* in relation to the old stereotype of "evangelism," which periodically gets redressed and recycled with the most sophisticated means and techniques. There is a crisis in *motivation* for evangelization, swinging from the old drive to "save souls from hell" to the appeal for psychological salvation through "possibility thinking"; from the "church growth" approach to the rigorous challenge of "radical discipleship"; from the apocalypstic anticipation of doomsday to the expectation of human liberation in history.

Perhaps the time has come to recover in its fullness the biblical perspective of the kingdom for the mission of the church today and particularly for our evangelistic witness. We have tried many definitions of our own regarding mission or evangelism. Why not try Jesus' own definition of his mission—and ours? For Jesus evangelization was no more and no less than *announcing the reign of God!*

(The above is from *Announcing the Reign of God: Evangelizatiion and the Subversive Memory of Jesus* by Mortimer Arias, Fortress Press, 1984 pps. xi, xii, xviii. Used by permission of Fortress Press.)

EVANGELISM——THE HEART OF
THE MISSION TASK

Evangelism is in many ways the heart of the church's missionary task. By pointing to Jesus Christ as the embodiment of God's saving action evangelism discloses:

* the reason for the church's existence,
* the basis for its faith,
* the central purpose for its mission in the world, and
* the hope which drives it onward toward the final goal of the kingdom amid the ambiguities of history and despite opposition and suffering.

The church's total mission in the world is unthinkable apart from its specific evangelistic calling to make Christ known and to exalt him as Lord and Savior. Yet evangelism is more specific and limited than the mission of the church.

Evangelism is the specific activity of making Christ known by word and by deed, especially to those who do not know him, so that all people may have an oppportunity to believe in him, to confess him as Lord and Savior, to become his disciples in the fellowship of the church, and to serve him in God's total mission in the world. Evangelism includes the call to repentance, the invitation to faith in Christ, and the promise of the forgiveness of sins (Acts 2:37–38). It culminates in baptism and the bestowing of the gift of the Holy Spirit for incorporation into Christ's ministry.

In evangelism verbal proclamation of the gospel to all sorts and conditions of humanity is crucial and assumes a certain priority over other expressions of the gospel. But it does not stand alone. Jesus came proclaiming the kingdom of God but also working signs and miracles that testified to the breaking in of the kingdom with power (Mark 1:14). He sat where the people sat and identified with the poor, the outcasts, and the marginal. The church's deeds of diaconic service, of healing and caring for the sick and the handicapped, and of advocating justice for the poor and the oppressed are powerful signs and witnesses to the coming of the kingdom. The proclaimed word often proves to be inadequate when not accompanied by the gracious deed.

Evangelism is the task of the whole church, of every church, and of every local congregation. Since it is preeminently the disclosure of the reason for the church's existence, no group of Christians can be excused from evangelistic responsibility. As mission is the *esse* of the church, so evangelism is the heartbeat of that mission—it expresses what the church considers central in its life. The Holy Spirit calls, gathers, and empowers the whole church and sends it into the world. Therefore evangelism is the responsibility of all baptized Christians.

(The above quotation is from "Perspectives on Mission and Evangelism," a report on theology of evangelism at the Consultation on Evangelism held by the Division for World Mission and Ecumenism, Lutheran Church in America, December 1983 and appearing in the *The Continuing Frontier: Evangelism,* page 97–99.)

HUMAN SINNED-AGAINSTNESS

A person is not only a sinner, a person is also a sinned against. Men and women are not only wilful violators of God's laws, they are also the violated. This is not to be understood in a behavioristic sense, but in a theological sense, in terms of sin, the domination of sin, and of our "struggle against sin . . . to the point of shedding our blood" (Heb.12:4).

We must not lose sight of the sinned-againstness of persons in our theological understanding and evangelistic effort. We must rediscover the horror of sin on human lives. There has been too much shallowness in our understanding of sin in the churches' evangelistic enterprises. Could it be that many evangelists in our churches today have no notion of human sinned-againstness? Could it be that in our much-cushioned life we cannot dismiss it as alien or only secondary to theological and evangelistic consideration? Or could it be that having looked into our own Christian experiences and found that our faith has made us prosper, we honestly think we are not the sinned-against, and so for that matter, that any one else need be the sinned-against? If that is the case, then no wonder the poor who experience indignity and injustice everyday don't give a hoot about our evangelism.

The Christian response to the sinned-against is compassion, not the popular unexamined notion of being sentimental and soft or pitiful, but in the proper sense—suffering with, fellow feeling, sympathy. Compassion for people is possible only when we perceive people as the sinned-against. If we look at people as sinners, we may have concern for them, affection or pity, but no compassion.

In the community of the sinned-against, something important very often happens—that in the struggle against the forces of sin, the sinned-against soon comes to realize that he or she is also the sinner in a way he or she cannot respond to with a "so what?" A community of the sinned-against struggling against the forces of sin is an evangelizing context. It is in a community in struggle that evangelism takes place. It is impossible to over-emphasize the importance of the community of the sinned-against in the evangelization of the poor.

When the poor are in the churches, to be pro-poor is not a political stand, it is a pastoral stand. Let us recognize the fact that most of the poor are not in our churches. For them, the evangelizing context is not individual encounter, it is neither a mass rally, it is far more personal and far more corporate. The missionary movement must build communities of the sinned-against among the world's poor.

(The above comments are from an article by Raymond Fung, appearing in the July 1980 issue of the *International Review of Mission*, a monthly publication of the World Council of Churches.)

FOR REFLECTION:

1. How does this reading relate mission and evangelism?
2. On a scale of 1 (poor) to 10 (great), how would you rate your congregation's evangelism outreach? The personal evangelism of your members? Your own witness? Why did you rate each of these as you did?

EVANGELIZATION IN THE MODERN WORLD

Confusion about the meaning of mission and evangelism began to arise when the concept of mission suffered a great inflation. Stephen Neill complained about the great inflation of the world mission, stating that when mission comes to mean everything the churches do, it ends by meaning nothing at all.

The Lutheran Church in America's "Call to Global Mission" participated in this broadening of the idea of mission by listing as the chief frontiers, in addition to evangelism, such things as poverty and oppression, peace and justice, intellectual and scientific work, and institutional and ecological crises. Mission becomes everything the church might do in relation to the whole world, and all these things are embraced by the term "holistic mission."

Instead of being a term which unites evangelicals and ecumenicals, it has become a bone of contention, each side claiming to be "more holistic than thou." Evangelicals fear that when mission is defined in terms of humanization, development, and liberation, or as a program to combat racism, concern for industrial relations, economic development, and agrarian reform, the classical meaning of evangelism gets lost in the shuffle. The church then finds itself mostly preoccupied with projects around the world at which it can only be second best, while devoting a decreasing percentage of its total resources in personnel and materiel to what she alone as the church, and that which no other agency in the world, can do.

Let us focus on the real controversy over evangelism. The controversy is not over whether the church should be involved in efforts to promote justice, alleviate hunger, overcome the uneven distribution of wealth, attack ignorance and superstition, stand in solidarity with victims of oppression, negotiate peace between tribes and nations, assist economically underdeveloped peoples—in short, create a better world order in which justice and peace prevail.

The controversy does not lie here, because people on every side of the issue profess to be in favor of a general improvement of living conditions for all who inhabit planet earth. All of these causes can be seen within the horizon of concern of the whole church for the whole world in all its dimensions. For the church lives in a world which belongs to God from its original point of creation to its final point of consummation according to the biblical vision of things.

(The above quotation is from an article by Carl E. Braaten, professor of systematic theology, Lutheran School of Theology at Chicago, appearing in *The Continuing Frontier: Evangelism,* published by the Division for World Mission and Ecumenism, Lutheran Church in America, September 1984, pages 32–33.)

MISSION IN THE WORLD

Mission is not a word for everything the church does. "The church is mission" sounds fine, but it's an overstatement. For the church is a worshipping as well as a serving community, and although worship and service belong together they are not to be confused. Nor does "mission" cover everything God does in the world. For God the creator is constantly active in his world in providence, in common grace and in judgment, quite apart from the purposes for which he has sent his Son, his Spirit and his church into the world. "Mission" describes rather everything the church is sent into the world to do. "Mission embraces the church's double vocation of service to be "the salt of the earth" and "the light of the world." For Christ *sends* his people into the world to be its light (Matthew 5:13–16).

(Taken from *Christian Mission in the Modern World* by John R. W. Stott. © 1975 by John R. W. Stott and used by permission of InterVarsity Press, P.O. Box 1400, Downers Grove, IL 60515.)

FOR REFLECTION:

1. What kinds of specific activities do you think Stott would call mission?
2. If mission does not embrace everything that the church does, what activities in your congregation would you call "mission"? What elements in your own life and witness come under that heading?

LIBERATION THEOLOGY

The prophetic nature of the Latin American Church has been both a growing fact, as witnessed to by Medellin, and a call to action. This latter is a call to insert permanently the *function* of protest into the Church's structure, the hierarchy becoming subordinate to the prophetic charisma. According to many, one of the most meaningful prophetic acts would be to loosen the Church from all formal ties to the State.

Gustavo Gutierrez believes that the Church's hierarchy should go even further, throwing all its influence, still considerable in many parts of the continent, against every dehumanising situation. Its denunciation should not be partial (individual acts of injustice), but global (the entire system of dependence).

The theologians of liberation consider this prophetic voice, directed to the world's crises, as the only way in which the Church can authenticate itself before a watching world.

One of the chief tasks of the theology of liberation for Gutierrez is to reflect on the relationship between salvation and the historical process of man's liberation.

Salvation is the key concept which explains the work of Christ as liberation. The biblical message of salvation provides a reference point for an interpretation of the signs of the times in terms of conflict in human history.

Liberation is the key concept which identifies the process through which history must pass in order to be rid of its conflicts and contradictions. It is the radical removal of all causes of alienation which prevent man from being fully man.

(from "Liberation Theology: An Evangelical View from the Third World" by J. Andrew Kirk, John Knox Press, Atlanta, 1979, pps. 29, 58)

MISSION IN CONFLICT

Perhaps the most significant fact in the history of the Christian faith in Latin America is that the "breath of the Spirit" has not only swept over the ecclesiastical authorities, but has also awakened a new life in the people. Thus the grassroots communities have been formed and number millions of participants, particularly in Brazil, but also in Central America, Chile, Peru, and in lesser numbers in nearly all countries. They are centers of community Bible study and of involvement in the life of the secular communities in which they exist. They are made up of lay people—men and women—who share everyday experiences in the light of the Bible, often under the guidance of priests and nuns, but otherwise of lay people; in some places non-Catholics take part. Here the trade unionist, the housewife, the university student and the peasant all meet and the result is *concientizacion,* a term coined by the Brazilian educationist, Paulo Freire, for "making aware"—creating awareness of the possibilities of wholly liberated people, and hence of the obstacles that stand in the way of achieving that liberation, namely oppression and economic injustice. The contribution they have made, not only to the community but to the whole life of the Church, moved the Brazilian theologian Leonard Boff to entitle his book on the communities *The Grassroots Communities Re-invent the Church*. These communities maintain in most cases a fluid relationship with the "normal" structure of the Church. They are accepted by the hierarchy and in some places very much supported and promoted by it—though sometimes they are regarded with suspicion—but at the same time they preserve a certain freedom and autonomy. In some ways the grassroots communities have created a new role for the Catholic laity who traditionally play a passive part in church life. Moreover, by providing the Church with a solid, conscious and active base in the poor population (to which the majority belong), they have enabled it to free itself from (or at least to resist better) the pressure of sectors of the oligarchy to which it used to be too closely bound. Church leaders have been able to listen to the voices of the ordinary people, with their simple but committed interpretation, and in so doing have been helped to hear the Word of God anew.

In Latin America, as elsewhere, the separating lines between Christians are no longer defined by confessional borders but run across them. The real division—and the real unity—is discovered and expressed in attitudes to the Church's mission, to poverty and oppression, to political and economic dependence, and to the cultural manipulation of the people. Among Latin American Protestants a growing number see ecumenism as sharing in the common struggle to overcome the conditions that lead to the oppression of the people. Confessional and ecclesiastical differences are not regarded as significant in this broader context, and the emphasis of ecumenical theology is on working together rather than on coming together.

(From *A Vision of Hope* by Trevor Beeson and Jenny Pearce, Philadelphia, Fortress Press, 1984, pps. 39 and 41. Used by permission of Fortress Press.)

FOR REFLECTION:

Some have criticized the approach of liberation theology for giving priority to political action over proclaiming the Gospel. Its supporters counter that you cannot preach the Gospel to a starving person without offering bread. How do you think proclamation and social action should relate in God's mission.

THE ROLE OF THE CHURCH IN SOUTH AFRICA

A Church that is in solidarity with the poor can never be a wealthy Church. It must sell all in a sense to follow its Master. It must sit loosely to the things of this world, using its wealth and resources for the sake of the least of Christ's brethren.

Such a Church will have to be a suffering Church, one which takes up its cross to follow Jesus. A Church that does not suffer is a contradiction in terms if it is not marked by the cross and inspired by the Holy Spirit. It must be ready to die, for only so can it share in Christ's passion so as to share his resurrection.

When you are a slave what you want most of all is to be set free, to be liberated. And so for the slaves, the most important word Moses brought to them was, "I will rescue you and set you free from bondage." You and I know that God did do this wonderful work—he did set them free from bondage. He helped them to escape from their slavery in the mighty act of the Exodus. So we know another thing about God—this God—He is not just a talking God. He is not like Bishop Tutu who was warned by Mr. LeGrange, the Minister of Police, "Bishop Tutu talks too much and he must be careful." This God did not just talk—He acted. He showed Himself to be a doing God. Perhaps we might add another point about God—He takes sides. He is not a neutral God. He took the side of the slaves, the oppressed, the victims. He is still the same even today, he sides with the poor, the hungry, the oppressed, and the victims of injustice.

(*Hope and Suffering* by Desmond Tutu, p. 86 and 51, William B. Eerdmans Publishing Co., Grand Rapids, MI, © 1983. Used by permission.)

MISSION AND JUSTICE

Justice is basic to the renewal of the Christian mission. For Americans who enjoy the greatest affluence of any nation in history, justice may not rank high on our agenda. It may shock us to learn that it is primary for most people in the Third World.

It may be even more of a shock for us to learn that tolerance of things as they are is running low all around the world. This feeling was well expressed by Martin Luther King, Jr., in a letter he wrote from the Birmingham jail to eight clergymen who criticized him. He said: "History is the long and tragic story of the fact that privileged groups seldom give up their unjust posture . . . We know through painful experience that freedom is never voluntarily given by the oppressor; it must be demanded by the oppressed."

There are those who take the point of view that men like Dr. King are disturbers of the peace: Had he remained quiet, demonstrations such as those which occurred in Birmingham would never have happened.

It is important to marshal these arguments for the cause of justice because most Americans seem to have lost their sensitivity to injustice. They cannot understand when people rise up to fight for freedom in the 1970's, forgetting that we did precisely the same two centuries ago. Julius Nyerere, president of Tanzania, stated the case bluntly when he wrote: "A man can change his religion if he wishes; he can accept a different political belief— or in both cases give appearance of doing so—if this would relieve him of intolerable circumstances. But no man can change his color or his race. And if he suffers because of it, he must either become less than a man or he must fight. And for good or evil, mankind has been created that many will refuse to acquiesce in their own degradation; they will destroy peace rather than suffer under it."

It is in this context that the issue of *justice* has become a significant part of mission in our day. Justice has always been a part of the mission of God's people, although a part that is easy to forget when we are materially blessed.

(Quotation from *What Next in Mission?* by Paul A. Hopkins, Copyright © Westminster Press, 1977, page 56–58. Reprinted and used by permission.)

FOR REFLECTION:

1. How would you define *justice*?
2. Why is justice vital to the mission of the church?

A CURRENT ISSUE: THE PHILIPPINE STRUGGLE

On March 2, 1986, two million Filipinos gathered in Manila's Luneta Park to celebrate the triumph of "People's Power." Mostly dressed in yellow, the celebrants carried banners, picnic baskets and a deep sense of pride in their victory over the Marcos dictatorship.

Some 300 miles from Manila, on the island of Negros, sugar workers were also celebrating. They had just won a four-month strike and a two-fold increase in pay. Even with the increase in their salary of $1.60 per day will not be enough to save their malnourished children from the pain, diseases and even death of poverty. But they had endured much for the victory; military harassment and months of surviving only on food shared with them by key sugar workers at other haciendas. They experienced their power, and renewed their hope in their long struggle against poverty.

In assessing recent events, some Filipino Christians point to the Magnificat where Mary proclaims that God has "put down the mighty from their thrones, and exalted those of low degree . . . [and] filled the hungry with good things" (Luke 1:52–53) Filipinos rejoice that the mighty have been put down from their thrones, but still they ask, will the millions of Filipinos who are hungry be filled with good things?

The Philippines: a land of contrasts. Bamboo villages; modern cities. Asian traditions; Western influence. Rich land; hungry people.

Four hundred fifty years of Spanish and U.S. colonial rule have deeply influenced Philippine society. Government institutions are modeled after those of the United States. Eighty-five percent of the people are Roman Catholic and nine percent are Protestant. Only the Muslims in the south and some of the tribal groups have resisted Christian influence. Coca-cola, blue jeans and "American Top-40" music are prevalent throughout Philippine society today. But beneath the surface, tradtional values remain strong.

Philippine food production ranks in the top 15 in the world. More than a billion dollars worth of food products are exported each year. Yet seven of every 10 Filipino children are malnourished. And 70–80 percent of the people live below the poverty line. Most do not even enjoy two meals per day of dried fish, rice and vegetables, two sets of clothes per year and medicine for only the most simple ailments. How can an abundant country not be able to feed its people? The answer may be found in the history of Philippine colonialism with its decades of poverty, elitism and social injustice.

(From *Prepare*, July 1986, published by National Impact, Washington, D.C.)

CHRISTIAN MISSION IN CONFUSION

A puzzling and somewhat ironic situation exists within Christendom today. Those forms of the church that used to be peripheral—so far off center, some of them, as to have earned the epithet "the lunatic fringe" have sprung to the forefront. They are full of vim and vigor; they dominate the media and the mentality of the general public; they do not lack for material support; above all, they have a very definite and confident sense of their Christian mission. Meanwhile, the older, established churches that in the recent past constituted that dominant and normative center in relation to which these others could be thought peripheral and sectarian have languished. They have suffered quantitative losses and seem uncertain not only what they are in themselves but also what they ought to be doing in the world.

We could become a significant witnessing community at a time of profound need in the affairs of people and nations. We could be made real. We could cast off the aura of unreality that clings to these old structures of ours.

The clue to our transformation, I think, lies in a new understanding of our mission, or, rather an understanding that, while it is by no means radically new, has been able to take into itself the unique and concrete realities of life in the nuclear age. This new understanding expresses its message in ways that can be heard by many human beings and groupings through whom God is already conducting God's mission in our darkening world.

(*Christian Mission: The Stewardship of Life in the Kingdom of Death* by Douglas John Hall, Friendship Press, 1985, pages 1–2.)

CHRIST CONFRONTS INDIA

. . . Christianity has hardly touched and hardly makes an impact on the great religions of India. This is a great challenge for the church today. . . . There is a definite need for rethinking Christianity in terms which would be intelligible to the Indian mind. Christianity's foreignness in the cultural sense of the word has to be overcome, i.e. it must become "at home" in India against the background of Indian culture without the danger of compromising its fundamental truths.

. . . There is a great need for change of church structure . . . (but) Indian Christians are very slow to accept and in some cases are opposed to indigenous experiments. While this might be the state of the church, what of the non-Christians in India who constitute over 97 percent of the total population of the country? It is encouraging to know from several sources that they have a healthy attitude towards Christ, but they are anxious to receive him in an Indian garb.

It is high time that we should change and introduce indigenous methods both in the existing church and to communicate the Gospel to non-Christians and thus establish "indigenous churches."

(By B.V. Subbamma, from *Spirit and Struggle in Southern Asia,* edited by Barbara H. Chase and Martha L. Man, Friendship Press, 1986, p. 85)

THE MISSION OF THE CROSS

Right from my teen age when I first read about the great Sadhu Sundar Singh, I have come to believe in the mission of the cross as most appropriate for India. This idea was brought home to me in one of the most telling episodes from the life of the Sadhu.

He writes about an occasion when he was travelling through the snowclad Himalayan ranges across to Tibet. It was heavily snowing on this particular day. A Tibetan Lama (monk) had joined him on his way and also in conversation. Before long they came upon a heap of snow with a piece of saffron cloth peeping out. Quickly they cleared the snow and found a monk trapped under the snow and he was unconscious. The Sadhu and the Lama still had a few miles to walk before reaching the next village. Unless they ran fast they might not save their own lives,

said the Lama. But the Sadhu insisted on carrying the unconscious monk to safety. The Lama counselled the Sadhu to leave
the monk alone and run for life lest all three die on the way.
The Sadhu said he could not do this as the spirit of Christ in
him constrained him to carry the monk with him. But the Lama
scoffed at the "unwise" Sadhu and ran away to save his own
life.

The Sadhu carried his precious load, moving in slow steps.
Soon he found himself quite warmed up in body contact with
the monk. After walking for about a mile the monk regained
consciousness and enough strength for himself to walk along
with the Sadhu. Then after clearing another mile in the snow,
not far from a village, these two found a heap of snow freshly
formed. On opening it they found that the Lama, who had parted
their company not long ago, was now caught under the snow.
Turning him around they found him dead. It was then, the Sadhu
says, he understood the meaning of the words of the Master:
"He who would lose his life for my sake will gain it but he who
wants to save his life will lose it." (Luke 9:24). And herein is
the way of the cross for our mission.

(By M. Azariah, from *Spirit and Struggle in Southern Asia* edited by
Barbara H. Chase and Martha L. Man, Friendship Press, 1986, p. 87)

ON BEING STEWARDS

What if now we cast aside our qualifications, our ambivalence,
our docetism, and declare in word and deed—as a matter of
Christian praxis—that "We Care"? What if this care became, not
just a sentiment, an ethic, a duty but a very way of *being?* What
if, in the midst of such a society, instead of showing up as a
well-known religious element going aobut our well-known attempt at saving the world from its moral wickedness, or winning
converts, or winning arguments, or influencing the powerful, or
just trying to survive (!), the church began to be perceived as a
community that cares for the world, as such, for its welfare, its
justice, its peace, its survival? What if, in place of thinking itself
as the dispenser of salvation whose task it is to turn as much of
"the world" into "the church" as possible, the Christian community began to act out of an avowed care for this world—care
which (it declares) it has learned to have in its encounter with a

God whose care for the world is infinite? And what if this community (not alone, certainly, but in company with all persons and groups of good will) began to think and plan and act and die for the preservation and enhancement of that "beloved" world? What if a religion that had acted out of the motives of service—not as yet another predecessor on the community of humankind but as neighbor to a species that fell among thieves? What if stewardship became our modus operandi, our characteristic stance, our way of being in the world—not an addendum, not a means to something else, not an evangelistic come-on, but the very heart of the matter?

(The above quotation is from *The Steward: A Biblical Symbol Come of Age* by Douglas John Hall, New York: Friendship Press 1982, page 138–139.)

THEOLOGICAL TRENDS IN THE CHINESE CHURCH

Christianity was brought to China during a time of feudal oppression and foreign penetration. The extreme miseries suffered by the masses of people marked the dominant theological thinking of that time with pessimism and fatalism. The world and life itself were regarded as dark and hopeless, dominated by Satan, and all non-believers were to be condemned. The church was very much detached from the peoples' revolutionary struggles.

The fundamental changes in the life of the common people brought about by the victory of the peoples' revolution thirty-five years ago have had a tremendous impact on our theological thinking. For many Christians new vistas have been opened for a deeper understanding of the nature and will of God, and new light has been shed for comprehending his words as contained in the Holy Scriptures. Divergent viewpoints existed within the church then, and lively discussions and even debates took place during the decade of the 1950s.

At that time, some people failed to take into account the tremendous social changes and they pushed some theological notions to extremes. Some Christians stretched the doctrine of "justification by faith" so far as to assert that Christians and non-Christians were two entirely different species of people whose ideas and judgments were diametrically opposed to each other. If the world does not hate us, but loves us, they said, it means we have gone the wrong way and have compromised ourselves with Satan. Anything true, good and beautiful in the world is but the doing of Satan who is "transformed into an angel of light." Some even went so far as to affirm that "God does not care about the question of good and evil. Human deeds are but telling evidence of men's hostility toward God. Christians must not only refuse evil, but must also refuse good.

But most Christians could not agree with those views. The controversies centered on four main issues. One is whether the world is dominated by Satan or ruled and overruled by God. While Satan lures people to sin and sabotages the moral order, God, the Creator and Redeemer, rules and overrules the world. All that is truthful and good comes from God. Hence all negative and escapist views about the world are not justified.

Second is the question of human nature: is it totally depraved or, despite original sin, does human nature in some way or other still reflect "the image of God?" Although "all have sinned and fallen short of the glory of God," there are still inner struggles "between conscience and flesh." (Romans 7) The Gospel is the supreme way to overcome sinfulness, but people, in general, act according to their consciences, and their good deeds should be appreciated rather than condemned.

The third issue is whether believers (church) and non-believers (society) are inimical to each other, or, while maintaining our unique Christian message, we can and should live with love and harmony in society. It is true that the Gospel is always something challenging or even a stumbling block to the non-believer, but justification by faith should not make us Christians proud and arrogant. The principle governing relations between believers and non-believers should be love, and only through love can we bear good witness to the Gospel and make ourselves acceptable to others in society.

Finally, the fourth question is whether faith and morality exclude each other or complement each other. This fallacy of antinomian ideas is completely repudiated. Faith and works should be integrated. God "loveth righteousness and hateth wickedness," so Christians should "abhor that which is evil and cleave to that which is good."

(Article by Rev. Shen Yifan, ministry at Shanghai Community Church, appearing in *Bridge*, a bi-monthly magazine on Church Life in China Today, published by the Tao Fong Shen Ecumenical Centre, Shatin, Hong Kong.)

IV. INSIGHTS

The sources and resources of good things to assist us in our exploration of mission are boundless. This section points to a story, historical reflection, words and statistics. Enter these items into your mental computer and permit them to help shape your sojourn in mission.

THE HOLY SPIRIT: THE EVANGELIST

When I was Bishop in Madurai I received a message asking me to go to a village which I had never heard of, to baptize twenty-five families. I went. And I sat down and spent a day with that group of people. It took some time to piece the story together, but when I had gotten a hold on it, it was a story in four acts.

Act One. A water resources team had come to assist the villagers in digging a well so that they could have a clean water supply for the first time in their history. The man in charge of this team was a Christian. He was not formally trained, even theologically naive. He was not good at communicating, in verbalizing his faith, but he made it clear that he was a Christian. He left behind the impression of a good, caring, honest, sincere man.

Act Two. Three or four months later one of the people of this village was visiting a neighboring town to do some shopping. A representative of a Bible society sold him a copy of St. Mark's Gospel; the man brought it back and started reading it. Now reading in an Indian village means reading aloud. So this man sits on the veranda of his house reading this strange book. And of course people with nothing better to do gather round and listen, and then start discussing. Week after week for several months you have a group of people reading St. Mark's Gospel, which is totally strange to them. Then try to make out what it's all about.

Act Three. Along comes what we call an independent evangelist. We have a rather remarkable breed of such evangelists in South India. Each one is totally independent of any human agency. Each one has a hot line to God and knows exactly what God intends, and they go around to villages preaching fiery sermons. One of these independent evangelists dropped in on our village, preached a fiery sermon and left behind a tract which simply said, "If you die tonight, where will you go?" Act Three closes with alarm and despondency in the village.

Act Four. The village decides they better do something about it. They will try to find out what this Christian faith is all about. They remember a village five miles away where there is a Christian congregation. So they write and ask these people, "Tell us what is all this about this man Jesus?" Now these Christian people are village coolies, day laborers. One of them had broken his leg and is unable to work, so his people said, "You go to the village, spend a month and tell them what you have." So he did.

And the results of these acts was that I was sitting down in front of twenty-five families of people as eager for the Gospel, as well instructed, as any group of people in that circumstance you could find. None of us knew about the four acts; no agency of the church had any idea what was going on. The strategy was entirely in other hands. I could do nothing else but baptize them, then and there.

(by Lesslie Newbigin, transcribed from an address to the Presbyterian Mission Assembly 1979, Kansas City.)

HISTORY'S LESSONS FOR TOMORROW'S MISSION

The Christian mission around the world today is in colossal confusion. There is no agreement as to priorities. There are those who give the first priority to church growth. Others would give the priority to the poor. Still others would see the priority as one of confronting the "prinicipalities and powers" of racism, militarism, repression of human rights, and economic exploitation. Then there are those who would focus on the needs of women and children. Finally there are those who argue that the most important priority of all is a fresh approach on the part of Christians to people of other faiths. Nor is there a consensus among

Christians as to which of the voices claiming global mission leadership should be followed. There are fundamentalists, the evangelicals, the ecumenists, and the liberationists. All of these voices can rally the support of millions of Christians on all six continents. It is difficult to make sense out of this global missionary situation. It is clearly a time of colossal confusion and untidiness. Many are tempted to despair of finding any clues that might help us to see where the Spirit of the Lord is at work in the churches around the world today.

If you have read Kenneth Scott Latourette's seven-volume study, *A History of the Expansion of Christianity,* you will remember that untidiness and confusion have characterized the great periods of mission expansion. There are, he writes, riddles to church history. There are periods when the tides of mission creativity and expansion have, like the ocean tide, run high. Then to be followed by other periods when the tide of missionary creativity and expansion has, like the tide, retreated with losses in numbers and vitality. Why some periods have been "high tides" and others "low tides" is never clear, he writes, but the historical evidence is unmistakable that there were those periods. It is his conviction that in all of the great periods of missionary history four things happened.

First, those who assumed leadership were people for whom loyalty to Jesus was a central concern. They believed in the Bible and loved the church, but the central focus of their lives was Jesus, truly human and truly divine. He was the One who had called and sent them. Historically, he argues, that is what explains these periods of missionary renewal and expansion.

Second, in those periods of expansion there was an emergence of new missionary communities that attributed their existence to the presence of Jesus in their midst. Again and again over the centuries they surfaced in the most unexpected places and among the most unexpected people, and from a historical perspective caught the established church of the day by surprise.

Third, in the great periods of missionary history numerical growth could be predicted but it would have been impossible to forecast in what geographic area and among what people it was to take place. There were always surprises.

Fourth, in those periods of church history when the missionary tides were running high there were always sustained efforts on the part of those who were involved in the missionary movement to influence the political, social, cultural, and economic environment. Their efforts to influence the environment often brought them into conflict with those in power.

(The above quotation is from an article by Tracey K. Jones, Jr. appearing in the *International Bulletin of Missionary Research,* Vol. 10, No. 2, April 1986, p. 50.)

A TWENTY-YEAR RETROSPECTIVE

The context for understanding Vatican II includes the post-Christendom age, the ecumenical movement, worldwide pluralism, the epochal decline in the West's global hegemony, and the rapid, powerful emergence on the universal stage of Asia, the Pacific, Africa, and Latin America. Today those regions hold 78 percent of the world's people, with 82 percent projected for A.D. 2000. The context is global.

Vatican II embraced all human history as viewed within the purpose of God. Thus the World Missionary Conference held in Edinburgh in 1910 and all that flowed ecumenically from it must be weighed. At Bandung, Indonesia, in 1955 the newly independent and developing nations sought a common forum. From it emerged the designation "third world" and the movement for "non-alignment." These and other notable events form the council's dynamic matrix.

In Vatican II, one sees that the *aggiornamento* of John XXIII proceeded in two basic but interrelated directions. Internally for the church, the council urged renewal, worship, reform, and ecumenism. Externally for the new encounter in global engagement, the council promoted dialogue with, mission to, and service for the world.

Between 1919 and 1959 four successive popes produced five papal encyclicals on missions. These incorporate and hold together the views of two missiologists. Joseph Schmidlin of Munster, borrowing from the Protestant Gustav Warneck, affirmed the aim of missions to be Christianization through evangelization and individual conversions. The Belgian Pierre Charles insisted that the missions' primary goal is to plant the church where it is not yet established. These complementary aims, evangelization and church planting, through the missionary encyclicals explain the nature and structure of *Ad Gentes.*

On December 8, 1975, the tenth anniversary of the closing Vatican II, Paul VI issued "Evangelization in the Modern World," the apostolic exhortation *Evangelii Nuntiandi*. It claims new ground, evangelization theologically in the mission of the whole church. Its complexities defy adequate definition. It includes proclamation, but that is only one part. It penetrates all strata of society and seeks converts. It permeates cultures. For the laity, it means evangelization and witness in society, politics, education, art, and the like. It must suffuse all life with the gospel—in short, it becomes Christianization.

Evangelii Nuntiandi relates the church's mission of evangelization to everyone: to the de-Christianized, to those of other religions, nonbelievers, nonpracticing Christians, and to all Christians (reevangelization). For the latter it facilitates that renewal without which a larger evangelization is impossible. Here, without referring to "missions," it points to the church's universal mission.

Responding to the growing volume of liberation theology, *Evangelii Nuntiandi* links evangelization to the struggle for a just society and presents a theology of Christian liberation. If evangelization "did not take account of the unceasing interplay of the Gospel and of man's concrete life, both personal and social," it would be incomplete.

Within the world Christian community, the great new fact of our era is the emergence of the churches of Asia, Oceania, Africa, and Latin America. In 1985 they hold 52 percent of the world's Christians; 48 percent are in the West. In fourteen years the balance is projected to become 60 percent and 40 percent, respectively. Since 1900 the ratio of Christians in the third world to its total population has risen from 8.51 percent to 21.35 percent today and is projected to be 23.82 percent in A.D. 2000. Even in Asia the Christian growth rate has outstripped population growth. The center of gravity for the faith has shifted and moves increasingly into what so recently were called "mission lands," and this is not to deny the presence of the "unreached 2.7 billion." The church has become visibly and tangibly universal.

(The above quotation is from an article by W. Richey Hogg appearing in the *International Bulletin of Missionary Research*, Vol. 9, No. 4, October 1985, pps. 146, 149 and 150.)

LOCATING THE "THIRD WORLD"

Officially I have been this newspaper's third-world correspondent for nearly two years. But more and more I have the feeling that there is no such thing as the "third world" at all.

There are certainly poorer countries, sharply different from the richer ones to be found in North America, Western Europe, and Australasia, different from Japan.

But a single entity called third world—dangling somewhere below the first (the capitalist rich) and the second (the Soviet bloc)?

Politically, the term third world usually refers to the so-called Group of 77 at the United Nations, the poorer countries that form the majority in the General Assembly. What they have in common is a desire to extract more aid money, know-how, and trade concessions from the wealthier states.

The Group of 77 actually contains more than 100 countries. Their big political vehicle, the so-called New International Economic Order, is stalled and virtually lifeless. The group's General Assembly resolutions can be and often are ignored. The group is also riven by its economic and social diversity. Latin America is 68 percent urban; Africa, about 30 percent. Latin America and Asia have leaped ahead in food production; Africa produces less food today than two decades ago.

Perhaps it makes more sense to divide poorer nations into oil exporters (Arab states, Nigeria, Mexico) and oil importers (most of the rest). Or into manufacturers (South Korea, Taiwan, Singapore, Argentina, Brazil) and primary-product exporters (Kenya's tea, coffee, and pineapples; Zambia's copper).

Is there a better term than "third world" to keep the needs of the world's poor in view of the world's conscience?

The Economist's Mark Malloch Brown has come to prefer the term South as having at least some geographical logic (although he apologizes to Australia, which may be south but is far from poor).

Am I, in fact, this newspaper's South correspondent: Its Southern correspondent, perhaps?

Yet "south" too, has different connotations for different people. It means one thing to an American but quite another to a Vietnamese or a Korean.

Generalities like "third world" may be convenient in a media age that demands short-hand labels. They can also be lulling and misleading. New ideas can require new words. I'm still looking.

(By David K. Willis, appearing in the November 4, 1985 issue of *Christian Science Monitor*.)

A Footnote: Defining the poor world, the developing nations, the undeveloped peoples, the blocks of political philosophy is difficult. David P. Young makes this interesting observation— that the so-called "third world" actually contains the "Two Thirds World"—the majority of people: a head-count issue, rather than economic or political power. Reflection on this idea of the "Two Thirds World" helps us put issues and problems in perspective. (cf. *The Speed of Love: An Exploration of Christian Faithfulness in a Technological World* and *21st Century Pioneering—A Scrapbook of the Future,* both by Young, Friendship Press, 1986.)

LANGUAGES AND "THE WORD"

Acts 2:9–15, Tells the story of Peter's sermon being heard by all in the crowd gathered to celebrate Pentecost day in Jerusalem. 1,950 years later, the whole Bible or some portions of the Bible have been translated into more than 1,300 languages.

One hundred sixty-two languages are spoken by at least 1 million persons each, and represent 99% of the human population. Twenty-five languages are used by 3-1/4 billion people, 78% of the world's population. These languages and the number of speakers in millions are:

	Language	No. of Speakers (millions)
1.	Mandarin (China)	670
2.	English	369
3.	Hindi & Urdu (60M) (Pakistan & India)	278
4.	Russian (Great Russia only)	246
5.	Spanish	225
6.	Arabic	134

(continued)

	Language	No. of Speakers (millions)
7.	Portuguese	133
8.	Bengali (Bangladesh & India)	131
9.	German	120
10.	Japanese	113
11.	Malay-Indonesia	101
12.	French	95
13.	Italian	61
14.	Punjabi (India & Pakistan)	58
15.	Tamil (India & Sri Lanka)	55
16.	Telugu (India)	55
17.	Korean	55
18.	Marathi (India)	53
19.	Cantonese (China)	48
20.	Javanese	45
21.	Wu (China)	43
22.	Ukranian (Mainly USSR)	42
23.	Turkish	41
24.	Min (China)	39
25.	Vietnamese	38

3,248,000,000 People
(78% of world)

Over one-half billion persons speak the next twenty-five languages, each having 11–36 million speakers. This list includes European languages (Polish, Romanian, Dutch, Hungarian, Czech), along with familiar languages of the Third World (Thai, Persian, Burmese, Swahili).

The next twenty-five languages represent 200 million people, or 5% of the world's population. Languages include Greek, Nepali, Swedish, Afrikaans, and Tibetan.

The next twenty-five languages cover just 100 million persons, or 2% of the world's population. Recognizable languages in the list include Danish, Finnish, Norwegian, Slovak, Zulu, Armenian, Albanian. The remaining languages, including the 62 additional languages (spoken by less than 2% of the world population) are tribal or regional languages unfamiliar to most North Americans.

GLOBAL STATISTICS

Out of the approximately 4.5 billion people in the world, 1.5 billion call themselves Christians. These include 800 million Roman Catholics, 250 million Protestants and 137 million Orthodox.

Three billion persons do not follow Christ. One billion of these live among Christians. Two billion live separated from any Christian.

It is reported authoritatively that persons are being added *daily* to the Christian community in the following numbers:

In Africa: 16,400 per day
In East Asia: 1,000 per day
In South Asia: 1,200 per day
In Latin America: 10% per year.

Hard statistics are difficult to obtain, but it is now reported that the Peoples Republic of China has between 25 and 50 million Christians. At the same time it is indicated that Christians in Europe and North America are *decreasing* by 7,200 per day.

It is significant to note where Christian workers are serving and the population they are attempting to reach. It is further significant to note that the number of national workers are more than ten times those from the outside.

	National Workers	Alien Workers	Population per Worker
Africa	373,469	57,852	249,278
East Asia	35,080	11,239	1,395,274
Europe	1,013,639	46,103	105,008
Latin America	180,967	72,745	47,575
North America	754,892	21,889	1,321
Oceania	55,163	11,274	7,913
South Asia	208,439	26,663	1,365,362
U.S.S.R.	60,700	30	3,997
World Total	2,680,349	247,763	

The source for the above statistics is the *World Christian Encyclopedia,* edited by David B. Barrett, Oxford University Press, New York, 1982.)

CHRISTIAN FREEDOM AND LIBERATION

Awareness of man's freedom and dignity, together with the affirmation of the inalienable rights of individuals and peoples, is one of the major characteristics of our time. But freedom demands conditions of an economic, social, political and cultural kind which makes possible its full exercise.

A clear perception of the obstacles which hinder its development and which offend human dignity is at the source of the powerful aspirations to liberation which are at work in our world.

Love of Preference for the Poor

In its various forms—material deprivation, unjust oppression, physical and psychological illnesses and finally death—human misery is the obvious sign of the natural condition of weakness in which man finds himself since original sin, and the sign of his need for salvation.

Hence it drew the compassion of Christ the Savior to take it upon himself and to be identified with the least of his brethren.

Hence also those who are oppressed by poverty are the object of a love of preference on the part of the church, which since her origin and in spite of the failings of many of her members has not ceased to work for their relief, defense and liberation.

In loving the poor, the church also witnesses to man's dignity. She clearly affirms that man is worth more for what he is than for what he has. She bears witness to the fact that this dignity cannot be destroyed, whatever the situation of poverty, scorn, rejection or powerlessness to which a human being has been reduced.

She shows her solidarity with those who do not count in a society by which they are rejected spiritually and sometimes even physically. She is particularly drawn with maternal affection toward those children who, through human wickedness, will never be brought forth from the womb to the light of day, as also for the elderly, alone and abandoned.

The special option for the poor, far from being a sign of particularism or sectarianism, manifests the universality of the church's being and mission. This option excludes no one.

The Myth of Revolution

Situations of grave injustice require the courage to make far-reaching reforms and to suppress unjustifiable privileges. But those who discredit the path of reform and favor the myth of revolution not only foster the illusion that the abolition of an evil situation is in itself sufficient to create a more humane society; they also encourage the setting up of totalitarian regimes.

The fight against injustice is meaningless unless it is waged with a view to establishing a new social and political order in conformity with the demands of justice.

Justice must already mark each stage of the establishment of this new order. There is a morality of means.

These principles must be applied especially in the extreme cases where there is recourse to armed struggle, which the church's magisterium admits as a last resort to put an end to an obvious and prolonged tyranny which is gravely damaging the fundamental rights of individuals and the common good.

The Value of Human Work

The value of any human work does not depend on the kind of work done; it is based on the fact that the one who does it is a person. There we have an ethical criterion whose implications cannot be overlooked.

Thus every person has a right to work, and this right must be recognized in a practical way by an effective commitment to resolving the tragic problem of unemployment. The fact that unemployment keeps large sectors of the population and notably the young in a situation of marginalization is intolerable.

For this reason the creation of jobs is a primary social task facing individuals and private enterprise as well as the state. As a general rule, in this as in other matters, the state has a subsidiary function; but often it can be called upon to intervene directly, as in the case of international agreements between different states.

The priority of work over capital places an obligation in justice upon employers to consider the welfare of the workers before the increase of profits. They have a moral obligation not to keep capital unproductive and in making investments to think first of the common good.

A New Solidarity

Solidarity is a direct requirement of human and supernatural brotherhood. The serious socio-economic problems which occur today cannot be solved unless new fronts of solidarity are created: solidarity of the poor among themselves, solidarity with the poor to which the rich are called, solidarity among the workers and with the workers.

Institutions and social organizations at different levels, as well as the state, must share in a general movement of solidarity. When the church appeals for such a solidarity, she is aware that she herself is concerned in a quite special way.

The principles that goods are meant for all, together with the principle of human and supernatural brotherhood, express the responsibilities of the richer countries toward the poorer ones.

(The above are key sections from "Instruction on Christian Freedom and Liberation", a document issued on April 5, 1986 by the Roman Catholic Congregation for the Doctrine of the Faith, as published in the *New York Times* on April 6, 1986.)

V. EDUCATION

From the time of the apostles, the faith has been transmitted on a one-to-one basis. The company of believers taught the beliefs to new followers. Continuing down through the centuries, Christians have taught and caught the faith, been taught and became teachers. Educational methods were incorporated into the evangelistic heritage of the church; evangelism became a part of the teaching model. So it is today: we are shaped by teaching and we shape through teaching.

E4M = EDUCATION FOR MISSION

Like mission itself, education for mission is an intentional activity. Its objective is specific, not general. Education for mission should be a specific, identified and priority emphasis in the congregation. Education for mission is not all Christian education; Christian education is not all education for mission.

E4M seeks to analyze, to provide information, to motivate, to suggest individual and group action relating to our "being in mission." Intellectually and emotionally, we are to be educated for mission.

E4M builds upon basic Christian education which teaches the faith, reviews church history, supplies Biblical information, and involves us in the Christian community. Being nurtured and supported for the Christian life by Christian education, E4M directs us "out", for others, to evangelistic efforts, to loving care and service. E4M needs to share information, but information leading to action. E4M seeks to undergird mission which is the church in action, reaching out in love and word to those who do not know God's love in Jesus Christ.

PHILOSOPHY OF EDUCATION FOR MISSION

The Program Committee on Education for Mission affirms the importance and necessity of education for mission. Mission is at the heart and center of the Church's life and through the centuries, people of faith have witnessed in word and in deed everywhere on earth.

Education for mission enables people to discover the meaning of mission; to learn about the church's involvement throughout the world; to prepare themselves for ministry in mission; and to engage individually and corporately in expressions of mission.

Education for mission can be defined as equipping the people of God so that they may widen their vision and invest their strength in meeting opportunities for mission now before them.

Mission

Mission is obedient reponse to our Lord and Saviour. The risen Christ commissioned his followers to witness to God's love for the world through word and deed. This commission cannot be understood apart from the story of God's action in the world which we find in the Scriptures of the Old and New Testaments where we hear the call to live in trust and partnership with God and to participate in the fulfillment of God's purposes in history (Acts 2:14ff; 7; 13:16ff).

Some dimensions of that call are:
• The mission is God's, in which we are called to participate. Isa. 42: 6–9, John 20:21b, Acts 10 & 11; I Cor. 1:1–3.
• Mission is our responsibility under the terms of the covenant established between humankind and God. Gen. 12:1–3; Ex. 19:1–20; 21; 24:7–8; Jer. 31:31–34; Isa. 61:1–3; 8–9; Matt. 25:21–46; Gal. 3:23–29.
• Mission is calling to live in a Christ-like fashion for the sake of the world and not for our own sake alone. Isa. 49:6, Luke 2:32; Acts 13:47, 26:23.
• Mission is inviting others to become disciples, to respond to the reign of God announced by Jesus Christ our Lord and Saviour. Matt. 28:19–20; Luke 24:48; Acts 8:26ff; Acts 26.
• Mission is engaging in the struggle and maintaining the hope that God's righteousness will prevail, liberating the human family from injustice, oppression and sin. Luke 4:18–19; Isa. 42:1–4; Amos 5:14–15; Micah 6:6–8; Acts 16:16–19; Eph. 6:10–13.
• Mission is to live empowered and guided by the Spirit so that our words and actions point to God. Matt. 5:16; Acts 1:8; II Cor. 5:20; I Thess. 1:6–8.

Organizing Principle

Education for mission is necessary because of the tension, incongruity and contradiction which individual Christians and local congregations experience between the gospel proclaimed and the realities of life in the world. Inappropriate ways of dealing with that tension are: to conform; to condemn; to retreat. For people of faith, the only acceptable relationship between the gospel and the world is to live in the midst of the world as ambassadors for Christ; to love the world as God loves it; to serve in the world in such a way as to witness to God's love.

Education

It is the nature of the community of faith to nurture its members so that they will grow in faith and develop the strength to confront the conflicting experiences of life both within the community and beyond it. The community of faith is itself a nurturer and teacher. We learn and teach all the time. But it is still necessary to set aside some times and places for intentional educational experiences.

Education sometimes happens through an individual's encounter with a committed person. It is often a group experience. It always involves relationships—within one's self, between individuals, among people. Thus the leadeship style of intentional education experiences is one of interaction with the participants— teacher and learners being partners in learning.

Education can help people and groups overcome limiting ways and move into more mature expressions of faith. Learning can be said to have taken place when learners are living what they say they believe.

Education is not neutral. It either helps to maintain what is or it enables people to anticipate and live toward new futures for themselves and the world. The latter requires an educational process which integrates awareness, analysis, action and reflection based on the assumption that we learn as we are involved.

For Mission

The middle word of 'education for mission' provides a necessary linkage and sets the direction. The word is deliberately chosen. As stated above the task is not only to educate *about* mission but also to educate toward the clear goal of active participation in God's cause as it is revealed to us in Jesus Christ.

(The above statement was adopted on Feburary 3, 1983 by the Program Committee on Education for Mission, the policy board of Friendship Press.)

THE CHRISTIAN COMMUNITY IN MISSION

(A "European Seminar on Education for Mission" was held in Aarhus, Denmark, May 1977. It was sponsored by the Commission on World Mission and Evangelism of the World Council of Churches. A small group of mission executives and congregational leaders spent several days exploring "The Christian Community in Mission . . . in a near and global context." The following quotations come from the seminar and should stimulate us in our exploration of "education for mission." Material is copyrighted by the World Council of Churches and used with their permission.)

"Education for Mission aims to produce *pathfinders,* people who are *sent* to find the way. The role of *being sent* is the mark of being missionary."

"For me, a missionary attitude is one which inspires us constantly to cross the frontiers behind which we are entrenched, to be put in question, to refuse to settle."

"But Education for Mission is not just a question of crossing frontiers between my world and the world of others. Within myself there are also two worlds; I must first of all cross the frontier within myself. But it is risky to step out of the zone in which one is sure of oneself and of one's faith, and to have the courage to confront what is unknown and totally different."

What is Education for Mission?

Is education for mission a thing of words or a thing of lifestyle?
Do we in the West, the North need missionaries from Africa, Asia, Latin America?
How can people's local witness be seen within the context of world mission?
How can those concerned about 'the world' accept their own local responsibilities?

There are Christians who are very much involved in questions related to their immediate sphere of life and who hardly look beyond; and there are others who are engaged in world-wide tasks, for the "third world", for "church and mission overseas", and who do not see the tasks on their own doorstep. It is of no help at all if one asserts and tries to prove one's priority over the other.

What is important are the approaches to thinking and action at the point of intersection where the immediate small sphere of life touches upon the big world-wide questions, problems and developments.

"Education for Mission must seek to produce an attitudinal change in us. A missionary attitude is not just one which opens up our geographical horizons and inspires us to take an interest in and feel responsible for what happens elsewhere. Education for mission prompts and leads us out of the closed worlds we inhabit."

The missionary frontiers to be crossed are *historical* frontiers in the progression of God's mission. Mission always is a new beginning. Crossing of frontiers is always into new situations, with new questions, new times. The fronts of God's mission are fronts common to the churches of both North and South, and also fronts common to the church and the world, to Christian and non-Christian alike. Modesty becomes a missionary virtue. Mission becomes communication with one's companion on the road. Mission becomes sharing in God's work.

Education for Mission is no longer primarily a transport problem (how do I bring the Gospel to the other person) nor is its task primarily learning how to mediate. It takes on the task of keeping pace with God's work in the world, and this can be done jointly and done well only if one's own *oikos* (house) has it own place *in* the Oikoumene. It is not a question of awakening interest *for* mission, but of experiencing and recognizing the "inter-est" (being in) *in* God's Mission.

"World mission is only *interesting* when people experience the fact that it has something to do with themselves, with the situation they live in."

"What have you *won* when mission friends are up-to-date in modern world mission, and yet are not missionaries to their own society? Are they truly up-to-date?"

"If Christians work with non-Christians in fields like human rights or economic justice, then the traditional friends may begin to understand something of the *new* mission. Or they may label such Christians *Communist*.

"Offer an explanation of modern world mission to those who will listen, but do not expect everyone to understand. Who understands Jesus?"

"When I give food to the poor, they call me a saint. When I ask why the poor have no food, they call me a communist." Dom Helder Camara.

What is a Missionary Congregation?

What is the gospel for people today?
What role does the parish play in education for mission?

The Gospel for modern man is really the old Gospel—joy, hope, justice. Are these actually to be seen and felt in our congregation? If so, then it happens—a real missionary congregation.

Only in an encounter with God's world outside of the church can the local congregation discover the missionary dimension of its faith . . . only in its taking seriously all people's searching for God.

Our security is in God—*that* is the Good News. We are free to risk living as servants to others—that is the meaning of "missionary".

How is a Congregation Helped to Become Missionary?

How do we help traditional church-goers discover that they, as well as those in the "third world", live in a mission field?
How is it possible to educate people to accept new ideas when they live surrounded by conservative structures and images?
Why is it that conservative groups carry the church today?

In Education for Mission, it seems to me, the question of *how* carries too much weight. *How* do we do it? *How* can we reach as many as possible? The question of communication, of mulitiplication is a priority. And thus the categories of publicity, of figures dominate us. But *what* is being communicated? And *who* communicates it? *What* does the missionary congregation we call for look like concretely? *Where* and *how* is it lived?

The human spirit keeps looking for ways to break out of the structures and images that imprison us. That's God's sign, and our children have shown it to us.

VI. BUILDING

Education for mission needs to be a part of the total congregational life, built into its structure, programming and action patterns. This section offers thoughts for incorporating education for mission into the total perspective of the local congregation.

BUILDING EXCITEMENT ABOUT MISSION

Based on the assumption that "mission" is a vital and integral part of the life of any local church, mission activities must be seen as a normal part of the life-pattern of a parish. In addition to specific programs or projects which can be labeled "mission," there is also, perhaps even of greater significance, the mood or atmosphere of mission which should permeate all activities.

Earlier, mission was based solidly on the "Great Commission" and was placed before church members by quoting Matthew 28:19—"Go, then, to all peoples everywhere and make them my disciples: baptize them in the name of the Father and of the Son and of the Holy Spirit" (TEV). Or, Acts 1:8—"You shall be witnesses for me in Jerusalem, in all of Judea and Samaria, and to the ends of the earth" (TEV). As useful, instructive and compelling as such quotes may be, people moving into the 1990's are not responding as formerly to such mandates.

A firmer base of mission involvement and action is to begin with God. God is disclosed to us in a manner that calls forth a natural reply. God loves; we love. God forgives; we forgive. God cares; we care. God gives; we give. God serves; we serve. God our Father, revealed in Jesus Christ, is the motive, the drive, the reason, the inspiration, even the content of our mission. Martin Luther said it this way:

I believe that Jesus Christ . . . is my Lord.
He has redeemed me,
a lost and condemned person,

saved me at great cost
from sin, death . . .
not with silver or gold,
but with his holy and precious blood
and his innocent suffering and death.
All this he has done that I may be his own,
live under him in his kingdom,
and serve him . . .

This is to say that the mission of God's people flows from the
nature of our God. We are not commanded to witness; we gladly
share the good news. We are not living by a law; we are giving
our "yes" to God's love. Legalism does not lead to mission, only
to conformity. The Christians mission is a happy affirmation of
God and of our servanthood.

This mood or spirit shapes the life-style of the local church.
Mission infuses itself into the web of congregational activities.
At each place, the mission dimension should be discerned. Think
of the typical activities of the local church and you outline where
mission should be.

• *Preaching*. Mood here is most important; a sermon need not
be explicitly "mission" each week, but implicitly it has to be,
for that is what we are about. Yet beyond mood there is a place
and need for specific "mission sermons." Where a visiting missionary, either overseas or national in focus, is available, the
sermon can be an exciting mix of "mission report" and scriptural
content. The local pastor is not excused from his or her own
mission sermon by using a missionary; happily blessed is a local
church were the residing minister preaches mission.

• *Worship*. Corporate worship is a major aspect of the local
church's life. How can it reflect mission? Worship resources
from overseas churches, including music, can deepen awareness
of the world-wide church. The increased variety in congregational worship suggests that litanies, liturgies, responses, prayers, art forms and other devotional tools can be brought in from
other lands, other communions, other languages. Christians of
other traditions and other places can contribute to us.

• *Teaching*. The various educational endeavors of the local
church can all be mission education opportunities. In significant
ways, mission concepts and learnings are creatively presented in
the parish education curriculum of most denominations; the local

church needs to understand these, encourage their fulfillment and assist the teacher or class in expanding this experience. Consultation with denominational education leaders will show how and where mission education is wisely included in resources already in use. Organizational activities—women, men, couples, youth, etc.—present excellent occasions for programs, projects, studies or special events to be bent toward mission education.

• *Fellowship*. "Family Nights" or fellowship events or refreshments or cottage meetings can be pleasant times for reminding members of the mission of the church. Food, games, entertainment and music can widen interests and awareness. The local church cannot honestly be only focused upon itself; concern and attention needs to be extended "to the ends of the earth."

• *Service*. The care and nature of the local household of faith is an obvious task of a local church; there are numerous methods for serving both members and local persons in need. Mission reminds us that service is also for those beyond our immediate vision: the hurt in city and farm; the addict; the victim of drought, flood or earthquake; the handicapped; blind; deaf. Church World Service, Lutheran World Relief, Catholic Overseas Relief represent organized ways for goods and funds to touch the world's pain. We should support them to the fullest. Consultation with denominational leaders will show other ways for direct service or indirect service by influencing government and business. Our hand and voice must be raised in the service of fellow humans.

STRUCTURES FOR MISSION

In the deepest sense, local church mission education is the heart of being and doing. This is the area of life that shows what is central and determinative for the congregation. It is mission education that says to us and to others that Christ is the center of our fellowship, that sharing him is the key to our calling, that here is how and where we differ from community or social organizations and clubs.

Where does mission education reside in the structure of the local church? There is not one answer for everyone, for every local church. The size of the local church, the number and quality of leaders, the size and character of the local community, the number and relationship to other Christian communions, the economic and social dimensions of the community, the history of involvement in mission by the local church, all these, and other factors, give uniqueness to the local structure for mission education. The local church will establish its own structure and pattern.

The following factors should be considered as a given local church plans for its mission education structure.

What suggestions are offered by denominational agencies for local structure? Such suggestions would not be blueprints to be followed without questioning, without modifying for the given local situation. Denominational suggestions can offer meaningful ties with cooperating churches and with resources and leadership beyond the local, a consciousness of a wider fellowship and helpful ideas for local consideration.

The local church should lodge mission education somewhere in its structure. Mission education should not be an option; it should be a required function of the local church. Some structure, sub-structure of individual, should be provided with official status for accomplishing mission education in the local church. Accountability needs to be determined. Visibility of mission education should be assured. To see mission education as everyone's task or failing to assign the job to someone suggests that it will be lost in the total effort or will not adequately be faced.

Determined by local church size, priorities, characteristics, leadership, etc., mission education could be structured from the following possible options.

(a) A committee on mission education. A group would be charged with the task of mission education. It might be called a committee, a task force, a commission, a board. It might be composed of three persons or 20 persons. This group would have the responsibility for seeing that mission education permeates the life of the local church. It would undertake certain activities itself and it would work through other groups or program units wherever feasible.

(b) A subcommittee on mission education. Again, this is a group charged with the mission education job. Depending upon local church practice or structure, such a subcommittee would be an outgrowth of a larger segment of the local church program, related to the Christian education committee (this would underscore the educational task), or related to the stewardship committee (this would tie mission to the financial support system), or related to an outreach commission or some other umbrella board.

(c) A person assigned as mission interpreter, coordinator or expeditor. One individual is given the task of overseeing the mission education or mission consciousness of the local church. If the membership is small, if the insight to the job is not large, if a beginning is better than nothing, then one person might be enough. This coordinator, even more than a group, must have some commitment to mission, wisdom to move among and with other structures in the local church, a low profile to ward off obnoxiousness and an ability to generate enthusiasm.

The ideas for being and doing, for causing mission in your local church, can be meaningful and useful only as they fit into your developing local patterns. Activities, no matter how interesting and appealing, have to blend into your life-style as a local church. Busyness, in and of itself, is totally unacceptable today. Activism demands knowing "who you are" and "where you are going."

PLANNING

After years of criticism and denunciation, the local church has come back strong as the center of Christian activity.

With all the inherent weaknesses portrayed through sociological analysis, the local parish continues to represent the church's best possibility. It is in the local situation that meaningful fellowship can exist, that lives can be changed, that minds can study and grow, that service seems possible, that outreach is a viable option.

With renewed energy and potential, the local church is seeking ways to be more effective, to conduct its life more wisely. One of the better methods to come into wide use is "planning"—a concept utilized broadly in business and government.

Planning asks the local church to examine itself carefully and to articulate its objectives. All too often the local church does not see itself fully: what is the nature of the membership, what is the nature of the community, what are the strengths and weaknesses of each, where do needs call for action? Rather than following program patterns developed 20 or 30 years before, no matter how dynamic they might have been earlier, the local church must re-state its goals so that a life-style for today can emerge.

The examination of the local church's situation and its statement of purpose, both of which can lead to a renewal of its programmatic task, are the products of the planning process. This procedure holds such great potential for the local church that it is suggested as essential for establishing the climate for "being in mission."

Every local church seeking to renew or recast itself can obtain helpful guidance from its denominational leadership. "Church planning" by any name is almost certainly a part of the service available to the local church from the denomination. A contact to the agency related to parish life should bring valuable assistance.

Few national denominational headquarters will submit packages for local church swallowing. It can't be done today! The local church will have to begin with basics (theology and faith-statements), from which it will create its own expression of Christian fellowship, service and witness. This mind-stretching, heartrending process is the requirement for today and the future. Local churches must identify themselves ("Who are we?" "What is the church in this place now?") and determine their program ("What do we do?") carefully articulating objectives, and then working out activities for fulfilling such, needs to become the pattern for local church operations as it is at denominational offices.

The work of Lyle E. Schaller is an exciting contribution to parish planning. Readers are urged to investigate any of his books, with special attention to the following (all are published by Abingdon Press and obtainable from your local bookstore):

Parish Planning (1971, $3.95)
Effective Church Planning (1979, $5.95)
Growing Pains (1983, $6.95).

STOP: EVALUATE

On occasion we need to take time to evaluate our mission education program. Learning from mistakes and failures of the past, we may be more effective in the future.

Sincere evaluation of the mission education program is a problem. We avoid such evaluation by assuming people automatically incorporate new learnings in their lives and by assuming that programs cannot be improved very much even if evaluated.

Too often programs are labeled as good or bad by one person or by those who plan them. Both learners and administrators must cooperate in organized evaluation.

Any program of education for mission should include time for evaluation by the participants. It is a way to find out if a person or group accomplished what was initially set as a goal. To make evaluation possible the goals must be known in advance. Without evaluation, goals are lost, programs tends to be purposeless, patterns are unchanged, inappropriate procedures become habitual and progress cannot be measured. Evaluation increases awareness of goals and results and enables adjustment of programs to meet needs that participants recognize.

Use these questions. Answer each of them with one of four answers: Yes, No, Partly, and Don't Know.

1. Do we have a committee or task force on education for mission?
2. Does it meet, plan, make proposals and serve as an advocate for mission in the church?
3. Is the committee representative of the church?
4. Does our church engage in long-range planning?
5. Have we developed an opportunity for our people to acquire a general knowledge of mission history and outstanding missionary personalities throughout the centuries.
6. Have we provided opportunity for our people to develop an appreciation for a knowledge of the biblical basis of mission?
7. Do we conduct an annual school of mission for all age groups?
8. Do we have a mission emphasis in vacation church school?
9. Are we helping our congregation to see the role of our denomination in the total scope of world-wide mission?
10. Do we have membership classes or instruction for new members? Do we include the importance of mission?
11. Are we challenging our people and giving them opportunities for response to mission?

12. Do we have a planned program for teaching mission throughout our total church program?

13. Do we have a growing mission section in our audio-visual library and do we encourage its use?

14. Do we have a growing mission section in our church library?

15. Do we project mission in an attractive way through bulletin board displays and printed messages?

16. Do we keep people informed about the church of Christ in the world-wide scene?

17. Do we have systematic training in giving to mission through our church school and church?

18. Is our church moving toward the ideal of giving as much for others as is spent on itself?

19. Does our church highlight news of mission efforts each week in our bulletin or weekly newsletter?

20. Is our congregation informed of our progress in mission giving, at least monthly?

21. Are prayers for specific missionaries, mission stations and projects a part of each worship service?

22. Are periodicals which interpret the mission program in the homes of our members?

You may add questions to this evaluation. As a result of this kind of self-study you may wish to make changes in your mission education plans.

VII. RESOURCES

This section is a listing of "mission happenings" which could occur in your local church and community. How can the ideas be wisely adapted to your situation? What other ideas do they suggest?

BEING PERSONAL

1. *Missionary Visit*. Invite a missionary home on furlough to your church. Give a wide exposure: worship, Sunday church school, meet with local church leaders, have an "open house" or reception, visit the ill and shut-ins, get a spot on the local radio or TV "talk show" or arrange for the missionary to record a series of media devotions for later airing, to be a speaker at a civic club or at school classes. Invite other churches to share in the events.

2. *Mission Speaker*. Encourage local church organizations to have mission speakers in the programming. Remember the national mission worker not far away who is addressing local mission situations. A member of a denominational mission board could be invited to share his/her insight from meetings and contacts. Jurisdictional unit staff members have experience in the wider mission outreach of the denomination; beyond asking such persons to "do their thing" for the local church, stretch them and yourself by asking them to help you grow in mission, to relate to you the mission of the church as their eyes see it from place to place.

3. *Former Missionaries*. Most denominations have a list or can supply the information as to where retired missionaries live. Such persons often represent a lifetime of service in mission to other people. As is being demonstrated almost daily, the "senior citizen" has much to offer the rest of society and should not be put out to pasture. The insights into people and cultures, into diverse issues which belong to a servant of the Lord after years of dedication, can be shared in a fresh way.

71

4. *Overseas National*. Invite an overseas national to your church; follow the same pattern of opportunities listed for a missionary visitor. Many nationals are studying at colleges and universities; be considerate in your invitation. Do not unduly interfere with their primary task of education. Some students represent an elite background; care needs to be taken in selecting such speakers. Request for funds or support should be referred to denominational mission agencies.

5. *Travel*. Many denominations conduct overseas "interpretation through travel" or seminars for first-hand exposure to other cultures, peoples, churches. Such contact with the "first-century Christianity" or the church overseas can be a tremendous mission education. The "story" seen and heard should be shared meaningfully back home, not alone with one local church, but with neighboring churches and regional jurisdictions. Excursions to national mission situations or programs, to colleges, homes for aged or children, inner city agencies or parishes, etc. can be developed for weekends or summer "travel caravans." Individuals or groups can participate in "work camp" experiences both in North America and overseas.

6. *Traveling Sales Persons*. The mobility of North American people is measured in many ways. Consider the traveling sales person or executive: many have territories which could put them into face-to-face contact with national mission projects or even international efforts. Encourage such persons to visit, when "on the road," these mission situations and then to report back. The person will grow and the local church will widen its perspective.

HAPPENINGS

1. *School of Mission*. An educational/interpretative event, half-a-day, a full-day, a series of evenings over several weeks, a special session in the Sunday church school or youth fellowship or women's organization. The event or series can be intergenerational, interdenominational, community-wide. Any and all types of educational processes can and should be used: lectures, audiovisuals, missionary speaker, book reviews, map displays, art exhibits, etc.

2. *Mission Weekend*. Plan a whole weekend around mission themes. The central event, congregational worship, can include the sermon, music, banners, etc. on a mission focus. The Sunday

church school, including opportunities for adults, can place emphasis on mission education using either ecumenical or denominational resources. There could be small Bible study cells; all might study the same passage, or explore separate selections for sharing. A family evening or festival could unite the parish in fellowship.

3. *Mission Retreat*. Any group of members, youth or adults, could gather at an appropriate location for a weekend retreat. Speakers, study materials, action programs and activities can be tied together on a mission issue or theme or country. Foods and games and songs and study could be intertwined into an in-depth approach. Adults might approach a controversial or probing subject best when a whole weekend is available rather than shorter periods of time. Use of speakers, films, books could lead toward deeper understandings.

4. *Family Night*. Combine food, fun, fellowship, learning with a mission emphasis. Plan carefully each part of the evening; include activities and interests for every age group. Remember the "singles" and others not normally included in "family" arrangements. The program format could take the shape of a Mission Fair, with booths and displays.

5. *Mission Sunday*. Plan an annual "Mission Sunday" for your local church. Let it be more than an invited preacher for the morning. Involve as many members as possible. Let the Sunday church school and other events reflect the emphasis of the day.

6. *Fifth Sunday for Mission*. Each year has four months with five Sundays. Put a mission emphasis on that fifth Sunday. Let the preacher's theme be on mission. Develop displays, special lessons in the Sunday church school, a pot-luck meal. Take a special offering and give to general mission effort or a special project.

7. *Progressive Dinner*. Plan a social or fellowship event designed to widen appreciation for other cultures. Let each "course" be characteristic of a different area of the world; let the background music be appropriate. Venturesome hosts might even dress for their area! Entertainment might be songs from the areas, or explanations of local customs.

8. *Dialogue Sermon*. Have a local church member share in a dialogue sermon with the pastor; or have the pastor or lay member similarly share with a visiting mission speaker. Congregational attention can be sharpened up by this method; extremely relevant

questions can be raised and discussed. Use this pattern in other speaking situations.

9. *Ecumenical Round-Robin.* Have well-informed mission persons from various communions share in programs or events in other churches. It will become amazing how much work we do together overseas or in certain projects at home. Insights and learnings gleaned from mission contacts or persons can inspire others beside the member church. Ecumenical projects, relationships or institutions around the world tie local churches together; these common involvements should enlarge and strengthen our understanding of the "one church." The Mission Fair idea might fit well into an interchurch event, with each local church developing a booth or pavilion.

SEEING IS KNOWING

1. *Bulletin Board.* Most local churches have a bulletin board for posting notices, posters and clippings. Use it for "mission items." Mount on color paper for eye-focus. Or, develop a section of the board for mission items, changing it every week or so for freshness. A "mission picture" of the week or month could be posted; pictures can be cut from magazines or books.

2. *Mission Bulletin Board.* If the local church is large enough, or interested/aggressive enough, devote an entire bulletin board to mission. Put it in a prominent location; keep changing the material for freshness and interest. A good way to keep the subject before the eye of the congregation.

3. *Posters.* Mission posters designed for a special emphasis or program can be modified or redesigned for continued use. Here is a project for a youth group: design mission posters for the local church or for some special event. Poster-making can be a project for a "family night"—for all ages. Posters can be accumulated over a period of time and made into an art exhibit for display in the local church, library, bank or department store window.

4. *Displays.* Using pictures, artifacts or other objects develop an educational display. This can be related to an issue (race relations) or to a country (India) or to a project (inner city agency).

5. *Art Exhibits.* A variety of art is available for creative use in the local church. Some denominations have traveling art exhibits of genuine, authentic art executed by Christian artists around

the world. These expressions of the Christian faith and biblical themes can represent an important witness to us from the Third World; it is one dimension of "mission to six continents." Collection of magazine covers or pictures or art illustrations can provide a source worthy of exhibiting.

6. *Banners.* Flannel and other cloth banners have become popular in many local churches. Where such are being designed and made, see if one or more could be done on a mission theme. These might be made especially for a mission activity and then retained for regular use in the church.

LET THE WORD GO FORTH

1. *Parish Bulletin.* It is the rare local church which does not have a Sunday worship bulletin or program sheet. Selected quotes can be inserted in the announcement section; prayer requests can be listed; mission news items can be shared.

2. *Parish Paper.* Most local churches have a parish newspaper. See that a mission column is started, or intersperse items. Such a paper can be an important channel for mission information and education.

3. *Local Newspaper.* Editors of local newspapers will use mission related news items, especially when the story can be related to a local church, event or person. Since the local church is related to far-flung efforts toward relieving pain, suffering and injustice, prepare news items indicating how the local church is serving or helping in the midst of crises or emergencies. When a missionary or national or church worker from beyond your community visits, arrange for an interview with the local press. Even better, if you have a capable writer in your membership have her/him prepare something for submission to the press.

SOMETHING MORE

1. *Missionaries as "Staff."* When local churches share in supporting a missionary, national or overseas, an opportunity is presented to keep the vision before the members. Whenever and however (Sunday bulletin, letterhead, etc.), the missionary can be listed as part of the "staff." At the annual congregational meeting an official written report from the staff missionary can be included along with all other reports.

2. *Mission Telephone Calls.* As a part of a worship service, banquet program or study session, place a long distance phone call and speak with a mission person. The cost for an overseas or long distance call is not necessarily prohibitive. Plan the call well so that each minute is effectively used, get input which is uniquely related to the distant speaker and not as easily supplied locally. Special equipment is available to amplify the call, or play it through the public address system.

3. *Church Festivals related to Mission.* Plan a Christmas or Easter service or party with customs and experiences related to many people. Food, games, music, dress, stories can come from another environment. It will lead to a sense of oneness which overcomes differences.

4. *Temple Talk.* Have a lay person present each week, every other week or once a month a "Minute for Mission," or "Moment for Mission," a "Three Minute Mission Tour" or a "Temple Talk." Call it by any name, but it is a few minutes of interesting, exciting reporting on what the church is doing in mission. This can be a top-flight addition to the corporate experience for the local church, something to help the mind and heart and pocketbook reach out beyond itself.

5. *Prayer List.* Develop a list of people (missionaries, nationals), churches, institutions, issues, causes. In a systematic way offer intercessory prayer for them. There could be a "mission petition" suggested for each week, to be used by individuals. Another "mission petition" could be included in each Sunday general prayer or in the prayer at organizational meetings. Related picture or article would be placed on the bulletin board or in the Sunday bulletin or in the parish paper. Let prayers include thanksgiving as well as requests.

6. *Inserting.* Printed materials from denominational headquarters or other sources, reproduction of missionary letters or quotes from books/magazines, can be used as Sunday bulletin "insert"—not alone on a Mission Sunday or for a Mission Event, but on any and all Sundays. These same items might also be inserted in the parish paper and mailed to the membership.

7. *Pick-Up Reading.* Most churches have some place where "pick-up reading" materials would be helpful for the visitor or person waiting. The church lounge table, the church office, the "tract rack" in the church entrance, meeting room, etc. are excellent places for a mission magazine or an attractive book. There

are several fine mission books with photographs which would lend themselves to this use. If you have a church library, work with the librarian in planning this activity.

8. *Mission Names.* Parish house rooms, lounges or the local church itself can be named after mission people or places. "Livingston Hall" can keep the members constantly reminded of a great mission personality. "Uhuru Chapel" blends in an exciting manner the Gospel's gift of freedom with the sense of personal and national freedom in Africa. Names can be changed periodically; they needn't last forever.

9. *Mission Calendar.* Develop a mission calendar on which are listed the dates of famous mission personalities (Carey, Xavier, etc.) and mission events (Edition). Birthdates of denominational missionaries and historic steps in mission can be noted. The calendar can be educational and a constant source of mission information and awareness.

10. *Postage Stamps.* Some stamp collector in the local church might develop a "stamp collection" related to mission. Used or new stamps could be saved or purchased to provide interesting insight and identification with another nation.

11. *Coins and Currency.* Representative coins and paper money can be placed on display, as with postage stamps. New interest and sensitivity can grow from such collections.

12. *Hosting the Missionary.* When the local church receives a mission speaker, hosting such a person can be in itself an effective mission interpretation operation. Assuming it is not too much for the visitor's strength or interest, have him/her stay in a different home each night and take lunch and dinner in different homes—do not always place the visitor in a "mission-minded" family. Try the opposite.

13. *Questions/Discussion.* Whatever mission speaker you have, place him/her into a conversational setting for best results. Count on questions and comments to set the agenda and place. The message content will thus match the interests of the hearers; human interest insights can be brought home to the local scene more dramatically. "Conversations" with the visiting mission person might well be a pattern for the visit: morning and afternoon talks with women, children and youth; evenings with church leaders, women and men and couples. Many a mission speaker, not exactly at home at a podium, could wow a smaller group in an informal circumstance.

14. *Money*. It is through financial support that members of the local church become personally involved in mission. Tell that story. Indicate how much of the local church budget goes for mission effort. (You might have to dig for this data, but it is available and highly enlightening.) Search out how much and how far your mission dollars go: they could be larger and more effective than imagined! Many local churches do not support adequately or eagerly the mission effort beyond their own local program. Raise sights; encourage vision; illustrate involvements.

15. *Mission Projects*. There are opportunities for the activist to work for mission. Projects for children and women are suggested by Church World Service and Lutheran World Relief. Most mission agencies produce lists of projects for local church fulfillment; write and ask about them. It is always wise to undertake a project having some official approval, else the cost and effort might be unnecessarily wasted. Projects requiring money donations would, of course, be undertaken only after fully meeting the denominational budget quota.

16. *Local Service Club*. Try and get a mission message to the local Lions, Rotary, Kiwanis, etc. The right mission speaker, whether an outsider or a local person with knowledge, could do a real service here. If they use films for programming, an effective mission film could fit in nicely.

CHURCH GROUPINGS

1. *Parish Organizations*. Every local church has its own style and kind of organizations: youth, men, women, couples, senior citizens, choirs, etc. Whatever the local church has, and as much as they have, the programming of the groups can include mission thrusts, Book reviews, audio-visuals, speakers, social activities, panel presentations and many methods can be used to present mission material to the members. Friendship Press resources are designed for such structures in the local church.

2. *Sunday Church School*. The leadership of every Sunday church school should be alert to see that every mission contact or emphasis in the denominational educational curriculum is utilized. A mission-minded teacher could find many places for mission illustration and special attention. Someone in the local church could be given the task of feeding mission material to teachers; it means both knowing the curriculum well and having proper mission information to share.

3. *Vacation Church School*. Utilizing denominational mission material, one Pennsylvania congregation prepared a full week's vacation school program on world mission. Creative persons could do this with national missions and mission issues. Friendship Press resources would be helpful here. Denominational VCS material can be adjusted or modified to include a section or unit on mission. If this is done each year, a mission-mindedness will affect both the children and their parents—the whole congregation will be enlivened.

4. *Confirmation Classes*. Confirmation classes, adult membership class or whatever the local church has for youth preparing the membership, offer an opportunity to instill a mission attitude. Faith can be taught and confessed as something to be shared, as the foundation for the worldwide church of Christ. The excitement of new Christians in other cultures can help youth see the dynamic of really accepting their own "new birth."

5. *Study Group*. The small group movement is one of the signs of church renewal. Start such a group around a study of a basic mission text. As they probe the meaning and ways of mission strategy for both national and overseas endeavors, they will find provocative parallels for local mission.

6. *Work with Key Leaders*. Some materials and programs are meant for the average members, the large numbers. Other items can be more effective presented to key leaders of the local church. See that the denominational mission magazine or annual report is given to the leadership group. Let a given mission visitor spend time with leaders. Develop the "core" of the local church into mission awareness: it will permeate the whole. Leaders to keep in mind: the session, church council or general board; Sunday school superintendent or director; women's organizations, youth fellowships, worship or music people, etc.

7. *Special Audience*. Members of the local Christian community which might have special interest and receptivity toward the entire area of mission. Too often the aged and shut-ins are forgotten (indeed, this segment of our population represent a mission or issue overlooked much too long). Why not have the visiting mission speaker make a few house calls and share the message? Sometimes the visited can become an effective communication channel, telling many about the special visit they received. Young people might carry a cassette of a mission speaker to the shut-in. The faith and experience of these older people can prove highly significant to the younger church member seeking identity.

8. *College Students.* The local church's ministry is addressed to members away from home at college or university (also, those in the armed forces). How can "mission awareness" be maintained for this important group? Send the denomination's mission magazine to the students. Give students a mission book for Christmas; select a book with special relevance for the student reader.

SPECIAL MATERIALS

1. *Mission File.* Develop a file system into which pictures, clippings, references and other items are placed. Folders can be started on nations where your denomination has current work, on agencies undertaking mission work, on areas of the country or world which deserve your attention, on issues or concerns which face your mission program. Besides the obvious church publications, use secular sources for items to be place in the file: *Time, Newsweek, National Geographic, World Press Review,* newspapers, etc. Place effort on the utilization of the "mission file"—it is not enough to collect the material! Encourage leaders to tap this source for background on a program or topic; have Sunday church school teachers dip into this file; use the material for displays or bulletin boards; use the material in "quotes" for worship bulletins or parish papers.

2. *Parish Library.* The local church probably has a library and members could be encouraged to read the books. Such a library ought to have a "mission section"—books and magazines for individual reading and for reference. The books quoted in this volume form a good basic beginning and Friendship Press offers more suggestions.

3. *Pictures.* Keep a file of mission pictures, black and white and full-color pictures of people and situations and projects can be obtained. They will make the story real and exciting. Denominational offices could be of help here. Put a picture on the bulletin board; change it each week or so. What about a mission picture each week or month for every Sunday church school class (or room)? A learning story or a prayer can be associated with the picture. Let the pictures reflect joy and dignity, as well as poverty and suffering.

4. *Audio-Visuals.* Use audio-visuals on mission in the life of the local church. Include in this area: films, filmstrips, slides,

recordings, cassettes, etc. Check with your denomination (including regional jurisdictional unit) and see how films and filmstrips are distributed. Filmstrips worthy of repeated showing should be purchased and placed in a parish library; the same for recordings and cassettes. Films are not just entertainment; they require careful planning so that they are a part of an educational experience. Investigate video material, borrowing local equipment if the congregation does not own a VCR. Wise use of an accompanying utilization guide is strongly encouraged.

5. *Music*. Mission-minded persons, or those responsible for mission education, should help a local church keep mission in its music program. Numerous folk-songs relate themes directly or indirectly tied to mission ideas. Use of recordings of music from overseas; your denominational mission agency might offer assistance here. Mission hymns might be sung at meetings other than when a missionary is speaking.

6. *Missionary Letters*. Many missionaries write a periodic letter for distribution to family and friends; it is an efficient way to keep in touch with a large number of people. A local church could aid the missionary by offering to mail the letter: maintaining a mailing list, reproducing the letter and mailing it. Those receiving such letters should use them for mission education: post them on the bulletin board, duplicate them for distribution among the local church members, quote from them in the Sunday bulletin or parish paper. When being duplicated, information of a personal nature should be omitted; where policy matters arise, it is helpful to confer with mission agencies. The letters can be filed and used later as resource material. Why not have one or more persons respond to missionary letters: The mails go two ways and fellowship can be maintained.

MISSION PERIODICALS

Many denominations, mission agencies, and mission-related groups produce exciting periodicals which deserve attention and utilization beyond their normal audience or membership. The following list identifies such periodicals which you may find useful in your congregation. It may be that a number of congregations (in ecumenical setting) could subscribe and share to a cluster of these periodicals. Magazines of priority interest are marked with double asterisk (**). Your church library may be encouraged to subscribe to some of these.

Christianity and Crisis, P. O. Box 1308-C, Fort Lee, New Jersey 07024. $21. (A semi-monthly Christian journal of opinion.)

Evangelical Missions Quarterly, a publication of the Evangelical Foreign Missions Association and the Interdenominational Foreign Mission Association, Box 794, Wheaton, Illinois 60189. $11.95 a year.

**International Bulletin of Missionary Research,* P. O. 1308-E, Fort Lee, New Jersey 07024. $14. (A quarterly mission journal published by the Overseas Ministries Study Center in Ventnor, New Jersey.)

International Review of Mission, a quarterly journal of the Commission on World Mission and Evangelism of the World Council of Churches, 150 Route de Ferney, P. O. Box 66, 1211 Geneva 20, Switzerland. $15.

Missiology, an international quarterly review published by the American Society of Missiology, 616 Walnut Avenue, Scottdale, Pennsylvania 15683. $15.

New Internationaliṣt, (a monthly magazine for the people, the ideas, the action in the fight for world development), 113 Atlantic Avenue, Brooklyn, New York 11201. $25 a year.

New World Outlook, A monthly mission magazine of the United Methodist Church Service Center, 7820 Reading Road, Cincinnati, OH 45237. $7. a year.

**One World,* World Council of Churches, 150 Route de Ferney, P. O. Box 66, 1211 Geneva 20, Switzerland. (A monthly magazine of the World Council of Churches.) $14. a year.

Sojourners (An independent Christian monthly addressing political issues.) Available from Sojourners, Box 29272, Washington D.C. 20017. $18. per year.

The Ecumenical Review, Quarterly journal of the World Council of Churches, 150 Route de Ferney, P. O. Box 66, 1211 Geneva 20, Switzerland. $15.

World Encounter, quarterly magazine of the Division for World Mission and Ecumenism, Lutheran Church in America, 2900 Queen Lane, Philadelphia, PA 19129. $6.

Worldmission, (A quarterly review published by the Society for the Propagation of the Faith in the U.S.) 366 Fifth Avenue, New York, New York 10001. $5.

**World Press Review,* (Monthly news and views from the foreign press) Box 915, Farmingdale , New York 11737. $24.95.

Worldview, Monthly publication of the Council of Religion and International Affairs, P. O. Box 1935 Marion, Ohio 43305. $25 a year.

MISSION NEWSLETTERS

There are numerous monthly or quarterly newsletters which relate to various aspects of interest and concern for mission interpretation. These should be investigated since they offer ideas and information frequently unavailable through other channels. Among the more significant newsletters are the following four.

A Monthly Letter on Evangelism. This informative and stimulating letter has been written over the years by the Director for Evangelism of the Commission on World Mission and Evangelism of the World Council of Churches. The current editor/author is Raymond Fung. There is no subscription cost, though a reasonable donation to WCC would be appropriate. Order from WCC: 150 route de Ferney, CH-1211 Geneva 20, Switzerland.

The Parish Paper. This highly useful and effective two page letter comes from the pen/typewriter of Lyle E. Schaller of the Yokefellow Institute. It discusses a variety of issues related to parish life and ministry. Twelve issues are mailed for $5. (US currency) to an addressee in the United States or Canada. Checks should be made out to "Yokefellow Institute" and sent to *The Parish Paper*, 530 North Brainer Street, Naperville, IL 60540. Request information on multiple-copy orders, if interested.

Context. This 22-times a year newsletter comes from the pen of Martin E. Marty, Professor at the University of Chicago, and associate editor of the *Christian Century*. It explores the interrelationship of religion and American culture. A year's subscription is $24.95 and can be ordered from Claretian Publications, 221 W. Madison Street, Chicago, IL 60606.

MARC. This monthly letter comes from Missions Advanced Research Corporation and offers perspective and ideas from a major evangelical study and research center. There is no subscription fee. Write and ask for it at MARC, 919 W. Huntington Drive, Monrovia, CA 91016.

MISSION INSTITUTES

Numerous institutes, conferences, schools are held throughout the year to orient missionary personnel, train missionary personnel and equip mission educators. Congregational mission education leader would profit greatly by involving themselves in some of these mission education opportunities.

An annual listing of "mission institutes" which provides data on many of these situations can be purchased for 50 cents. Contact one of the following three agencies:

United States Catholic Mission Association, 1233 Lawrence Street, N.E., Washington, D.C. 20017

Division of Overseas Ministries, NCC, 475 Riverside Drive, New York, NY 10115

Canadian Mission Council, 900 Parent Avenue, Ottawa, Ontario K1N 781, Canada

Three differing patterns of mission institute can be identified as having valuable potential for congregational mission educators.

Overseas Ministry Study Center. This institute is based in Ventnor, New Jersey, and has operated for over 60 years. Its study program consists of 3–5 day courses from mid-September through early May. Ecumenical in scope, OMSC covers an exciting theological spectrum: evangelical, mainline Protestant, Orthodox and Roman Catholic. Write for annual brochure and/or announcements. Overseas Ministry Study Center, Box 2057, Ventnor, NJ 08406 (Phone-609-823-6671).

World Mission Institute. An annual institute is held each spring by the Committee on International Programs of the Chicago Cluster of Theological Schools. The Chicago Cluster includes principal Roman Catholic and Protestant theological institutions in the Chicago area. After February 1, request information on the annual institute by writing to World Mission Institute, 1100 E. 55th Street, Chicago, Illinois 60615.

Summer Mission Conferences. A series of summer conferences around the nation address the two annual study themes relating to Friendship Press resources. Most conferences are one week in length, with several one day events. Programs listed in the above "Mission Institutes" folder or with the Program Committee on Education for Mission, Room 772, 475 Riverside Drive, New York, NY 10115.

RELATED AGENCIES

There are a number of agencies or programs which can be creatively related to education for mission efforts in the local church. The following three programs deserve investigation and involvement by every local church and community.

Christmas International House. This ecumenical venture provides home-stays for international students during the annual Christmas holiday. Single congregations, or clusters of congregations, can share in this holiday hosting. Information can be obtained by writing to Christmas International House, 341 Ponce de Leon Avenue NE, Atlanta, GA 30308, (Phone: 404-873-1531).

International Christian Youth Exchange. This ecumenical high school youth exchange brings students to North America from countries around the world. The program is geared to the local church as host. American students can participate in a reciprocal dimension of the exchange by spending the summer abroad. For information write to ICYE, 134 W. 26 Street, New York, NY 10001 (Phone: 212-206-7307).

VIII. IDEAS

Letting your imagination move freely will surface a number of other possibilities. This section suggests other frameworks and patterns for consideration by congregations and communities. See if they can be adapted: see if they suggest other ideas.

ECUMENICAL SETTING

One of the more exciting aspects of the Ecumenical Movement is its origin. The Movement came out of "foreign mission" efforts of the Protestant churches. The first ecumenical conclave was the meeting in Edinburgh, Scotland in 1910; it was in effect an international gathering of mission people. The commission to be about mission was the cause which brought church leaders together to contemplate their oneness.

Facing overwhelming numbers of people, often hostile, missionaries from Europe and North America to the traditional "fields" of Asia, Africa and Latin America joined in fellowship and work. Early missionaries have to a great extent become the common heritage of all: Xavier, Carey, Livingston, Judson, Moffat, Schweitzer, Morrison, Mott. Confessional backgrounds, not ignored, have nevertheless receded in importance as Christians united in mission.

Ecumencial ventures have grown and thrived. In medical work there is Vellore and Ludhiana in India. In educational effort there is International Christian University in Tokyo and Pacific Theological College in Fiji. In mass communications there is the World Association for Christian Communication. There is the one mission in the United Mission to Nepal. Christians do work together effectively in mission.

The scene is the same in North America. In countless local councils of churches, local Christian groups unite in witness and service. Church World Service brings most Protestants into a common effort of worldwide relief. Ministry in the National Parks is conducted jointly. The interchange of ideas and plans and programs mark the cooperative life of denominations.

Mission education is a logical place for ecumenical association in the local community. Lack of leadership, small numbers, few missionaries and nationals, suggest that it is practical to join in facets of mission education. The joint work in North America and around the world indicates that cooperation is possible, even desirable. Local churches of different communions could find a new source of identity, a new sense of purpose by joining in mission study.

Every idea for mission education in the local church suggested in this book could be accomplished jointly by two or more churches. Beyond learning and thinking together, joint mission education could enlarge minds and hearts to the reality of "one world in mission."

Here is a list of ways local churches can cooperate in mission education. Can you add to the list?

(1) Churches join in "hosting" a missionary or national speaker.
(2) Churches join in viewing and studying a mission film.
(3) Churches join in mission study programs.
(4) Churches join in holding a "Mission Festival."
(5) Churches share among each other mission publications and books.
(6) Pulpit exchange based on mission theme.
(7) Churches join in preparing a mission display for the community.
(8) Churches join, inviting the community's cooperation, in a clothing drive or other service project.
(9) Churches join in hosting overseas college/university students through the Christmas International House program over the Christmas–New Year's holiday.
(10) Churches join in a high school exchange project, working through the International Christian Youth Exchange.

DOUBLE MISSIONING

A chain of events led one local midwest church to recommitment to mission. An inner city pastor told them of renewal in an urban ghetto; a national from Taiwan, studying at the local college, visited one Sunday and witnessed to the meaning of Christ in his life; a businessman traveled to Sao Paulo, Brazil, and came in contact with a dynamic Christian fellowship there; the youth group spent a weekend working with a home for senior citizens; a young member away to college shared in an ecumenical Work Camp in Europe; the women of the church got a vision from a special study program on South Africa. New ideas, new information, new experiences, all interrelated to the life of the one local church led to a group sense of dedication to mission.

What should happen? Be content with inspiration, warm feelings? The church determined to "double their mission response." They took some very specific steps.

(a) They doubled the number of "mission books" in the congregational library. (Fourteen boks were still not many, of course; the new seven represented high quality compared to cast-offs in the first seven.)

(b) Efforts were made to increase subscriptions to the denominational mission magazine. Subscribers rose from five to seventeen. And four individuals, along with the congregational library, started receiving, and reading, a mission magazine from another denomination.

(c) The church's budget was redesigned to carry 120 percent of their "load" for the conference. An additional 10 percent was designated for other mission projects.

(d) An overseas effort and/or person, were included in the church's petitions each Sunday morning. Such prayers were also included in organizations' devotional periods.

(e) Each congregational organization redesigned its program format to include stronger focus on mission education resources. A goal was set for at least one meeting per year for a national mission project and one for an overseas effort. Leaders in the Sunday church school began collecting information and materials to be interwoven as illustrations into regular curricula.

(f) The editor of the parish newspaper starting placing a mission item in each issue of the monthly. Quotes and "fillers" were used in the Sunday bulletin. Letters from missionaries, quotations from books, pictures of interest were placed on the church bulletin board and in classrooms.

(g) The church deacons appointed a subcommittee on mission, relating it to the parish committee on "corporate life." The group of three persons was asked to keep the cause of mission before the congregation, utilizing the regular organization and program channels.

(h) The choir director began seeking out music from overseas, or items with special mission content, for both the adult and children choirs. Liturgies, litanies, prayers and other worship forms were gleaned from overseas and ecumenical sources and utilized in the local church worship.

DOING WHAT I CAN

The mission speaker has sparked your imagination. Or, the sermon has stirred you toward action. The film has shown vividly the need of human beings in a specific situation. Where are the handles? What can you do?

All too often, both the mission speaker and the listener are content to be "inspired" and then move along as before. A response is required. Here are four aspects of a meaningful response to mission inspiration.

(1) Be informed. How frequently we do not even know where in the world our speaker comes from or has served! Can we distinguish between Nigeria, Liberia, Siberia and Algeria? Where are Guyana, New Guinea or Guinea? Examine a map, read a book, select the right TV program, converse with an overseas visitor. Learn about the world, about its problems. Be interested enough to be informed.

(2) Pray. The private "closet," the personal "prayer list," the intimate association through intercessionary prayer is part of our response to mission. Prayer should be a natural and effective involvement in mission. The life of a local church should be permeated with "mission prayer."

(3) Provide support. Financial contributions are part of our response. Every local church should be supporting fully its apportioned share in the mission budget of the denomination. The local church normally channels this major "mission support" through a regional jurisdiction, e.g., district, conference, synod, diocese. A good number of local churches do not support *fully* the total work of their denomination through this general apportionment or benevolence; but this is the major financial response to mission! After fulfilling this task, local churches and individuals can find additional channels; denominational oppor-

tunities and other worthy "causes" are available. "Your heart will always be where your riches are." (Matt. 6:21 TEV) Your bankbook or checkbook continues to reflect your values, to indicate your response to mission.

(4) Evangelize. You have become excited about the Gospel changing lives, making people new and whole. The story is not alone about these happenings in some faraway land (though, indeed, it occurs there, too), or in a state or province across the continent (though, indeed, it occurs there, too), or in a neighboring "mission situation." Mission begins with YOU: you are made new and whole, your life is changed, your values are readjusted. You become a missionary, charged to evangelize where you are. Mission response means being a missionary right here! *Being in mission!*

MISSION GIANTS

Over the centuries outstanding personalities have been identified with the mission of the church: St. Paul, Xavier, Wesley, Carey. A fascinating and effective method of education for mission has been biographies: the examination of the lives and works of famous people.

Several twentieth century figures offer insight into the Christian mission pilgrimage. A look at their lives can help us understand the recent past and dream of the future.

Among biographies or autobiographies which can stimulate an exploring group, the following should be investigated.

Crowded Canvas—Some Experiences of a Lifetime is a fascinating autobiography of Max Warren, who served as Secretary General of the Church Mission Society in England. His life covered a significant period in the twentieth century and offers penetrating insights into our understanding of mission. This book was published in 1974 by Hodder and Stoughton in London. Three chapters offer special insight to the broader concept of mission and would warrant study in a local church. These are chapters 7–9, pages 109–162, entitled, "Background to Office", "The Missionaries", and "The Ecumenical Movement."

One of the major personalities for the ecumenical movement and the Christian mission in the twentieth century was John R. Mott. C. Howard Hopkins has provided a definitive biography of this twentieth century ecumenical statesman. Entitled *John R. Mott: 1865–1955,* the book provides an overview of this long life and the contributions he made in world Christianity. The book was published in 1979 by William B. Eerdmans Publishing Company.

Lesslie Newbigin has been a major personality in twentieth century Christian missions. First as a missionary in India, deeply involved in the emerging Church of South India, he later became a key figure in the International Missionary Commission and the World Council of Churches. His autobiography *Unfinished Agenda* provides his personal reminiscence of important persons and events during this century. The book is published by the World Council of Churches and Ecrdmans.

These books—and other similar ones—should not be handled as "book reviews." The books offer personal stories, life events, historical and missiological gems, which could be discussed and evaluated for current significance. Have more than one person read the book, each reporting stories, themes, trends which provoke thought and stir reaction. How do they help our examination of "being in mission" today? See that your church library gets these books.

Stephen Neill is another of the great figures of twentieth century mission. Out of his scholarly pursuits, Bishop Neill wrote *A History of Christian Missions*, the sixth volume of the Pelican History of the Church (published by Penguin Books). The book was published in 1964 and presents an authentic and exciting overview of twenty centuries of mission. Easily read, the volume provides background to people, movements and emerging churches.

MISSION BY COMPASS AND OTHER INSTRUMENTS

The TV news, the daily newspaper, the weekly news magazine, the occasional conversation point us to issues and places that disturb society. The normal reaction or response is shaped by the news media or our prejudices/biases or selfish personal/national interests. How do you get below the surface, examine the deeper issues, see the Christian perspective? At least one thing is certain: you need more information than supplied by superficial data and one-sided evaluation. How do you get that?

One helpful method is exploring issues, places, causes in a group, learning new facts, interesting insights and conflicting opinions. Life is not simple; the issues require research and discussion.

Geographical Focuses

South Africa cries out for understanding. We need to investigate the background and current situation, since it is not part of normal North American understandings and not easily available in the daily newspaper.

Even simple investigation will surface numerous books on this topic. Special attention should be given to work by Bishop Desmond Tutu and Dr. Allen Boesak. Two volumes that offer insight into the church situation are: *The Church Struggle in South Africa* by John W. de Gruchy (Eerdmans, 1979) and *The South African Churches in a Revolutionary Situation* by Marjorie Hope and James Young (Orbis, 1981).

The emerging Christian fellowship in the Peoples Republic of China promises to be one of the great chapters of Christian history as the twentieth century comes to a close. The books and articles written on China are now too numerous to list. At the same time, it is possible to pinpoint several that would be helpful in grasping the Christian phenomena there. *Religion in China* by Robert G. Orr is one of the basic resources available (Friendship Press, 1980). Books reflecting the total situation in a country or area should be read along with those specifically describing Christians and the church. One such book on China is *The Gate of Heavenly Peace: The Chinese and Their Evolution 1895–1980* by Jonathan D. Spence (Penguin Books, 1981).

One of the most confusing areas confronting North American attention is that of Central America. We know so little of its history and have not reflected upon its struggle for independence and self-respect. A study by the British Council of Churches offers insights not only to those of the United Kingdom but also to those of North America—it is the volume *A Vision of Hope* by Trevor Beeson and Jenny Pearce (Fortress Press, 1984). The Latin American context for Central America is further seen in Mortimer and Esther Arias' book , *The Cry of My People* (Friendship Press, 1980).

Topical Issues

Whether North American Christians wish to face it or not, Marxism is one of the major theologies permeating the thought and lives of contemporary people. We need to study and think about what the critique and contribution of Karl Marx is to twentieth century thought, rather than just being "anti-Communist." A very useful resource on this topic is *Christians and Communists* by Ans J. van der Bent (World Council of Churches, 1980). This European author offers insights not normally available to North American readers. *Christians and the Many Faces of Marxism,* edited by Wayne Stumme (Augsburg, 1984) is a North American study seeking to provide reliable information as to the origins and contemporary expressions of Marx's thought.

Within the last decade a movement has developed to create a "new international information order" whereby the Third World would be more adequately and accurately portrayed to the world's public. Of special concern and interest to countries in Asia, Africa and Latin America, the new order seeks to balance a western or northern dominated presentation of current events.

Video Cassettes

As the 1980's come to a close, video equipment has become a common household resource and educational tool available to local churches. It is certain this medium will be even more significant in the 1990's. For individual persons, families, small groups, and even regular congregational groupings (perhaps using more than one monitor), will find video equipment an important dimension of education for mission. In addition to utilizing resources specifically produced by denominations and ecumenical organizations for mission education, some of the more thoughtful products from the motion picture industry can be used in educational settings. Let's look at two possibilities, recognizing that many others are potentially available for similar usage.

The highly acclaimed film "Ghandi" gives us an honest and intimate view into the life of one of the great characters of the twentieth century. It further introduces us to India and the problems facing that country following its decades of colonization. A group viewing of this video cassette would provide stimulation for countless questions. Where did Ghandi get his philosophy of life? How would we react to the pre-independent situation in India? How did Ghandi address the pluralistic religious scene in India? What examples or parables of life does the film present to us?

The interplay and the mix of politics, economics and religion occurs in many places on the globe. The film "Missing" confronts the American conscience with its involvement in the affairs of other states. A group viewing of this film could stir many feelings and ideas—all worthy of exploration and scrutiny.

Films, especially available to us in video format, offer more than entertainment. They provide insights into issues, peoples and realities not otherwise easily available. Rather than just being entertained, we should seek together their meaning for life.

Novels

Authors down through the years have captured the human experience in story form. Insights into people, situations, problems, cultures all stand out vividly for us as we follow the storyline presented by a novelist. Many of these stories probe deeply into human predicaments and social-economic-political problems facing peoples and nations. We should listen and learn from authors as they seek to guide us in our human journey.

The situation in South Africa can become more human and disturbing by reading Alan Payton's *Ah, But Your Country is Beautiful* or Elsa Jaubert's *Poppie*.

Shusakun Endo is one of the leading contemporary novelists of Japan. A teenage convert to Roman Catholicism, he seeks to explore the struggle of a Japanese to comprehend and accept the Christian faith. Among his more helpful novels are *Silence* and *Wonderful Fool*.

John Hershey has given us a fictionalized version of his parents and his own life from China. *The Call* is a contemporary novel worth individual reading and group discussion. James Michener's *The Covenant* provides a historical foundation and overview of the Southern Africa problem. These so-called "secular" novels should be explored and critiqued as we engage in the task of education for mission.

Books of Analysis

As China became open in the early 1970's, Ross Terrill wrote a number of books which aided their readers in getting a glimpse of China which had been closed for almost twenty-five years. Similar books are available to explore countries, peoples in all sections of the globe. Capturing personal insights, these books make real to us places and people, even beyond that which a personal trip might provide. An excellent example is David Shipler's *Russia* (Penguin Books, 1983). This New York Times reporter reflects upon his four years in Moscow, offering a journalist's memoir at its best.

David Lamb, following four years in Nairobi with the Los Angeles Times, produced *The Africans* (Vintage Books, 1983). His story-telling and reporting of Africa provides insights and critique invaluable in understanding this important continent and its destiny for the immediate future.

The Japanese Mind by Robert C. Christopher (Fawcett Columbine Book, 1983) and *The Japanese* by Edwin O. Reischauer (Harvard Press, 1977) offer eye-opening perspectives on a people and nation which too often is only mysterious and beyond comprehension for North Americans.

Books as indicated above—and there are numerous others besides—offer a critical and analytical overview of people and lands which we desperately need. Reading them as individuals and discussing them in groups will stretch our minds and improve our sense of being in mission.

BULLETIN INSERTS: DO-IT-YOURSELF!

Bulletin Inserts are single sheets of paper, varied in size, style and color, which convey an important, attention-getting, limited-scope short message. The *Insert* is stuffed into a Sunday church bulletin—or used as an enclosure in church-letters, or an attachment to a parish newspaper.

Bulletin Inserts are among the most widely read church "literature," conveying a multitude of messages and concerns to the members of congregations. *Bulletin Inserts* seek to provide information, to change attitudes and opinions, to suggest action patterns, to inspire and motivate. *Bulletin Inserts* have been around for a long time! They are bound to be around even longer!

The usual, even normal, sources for *Bulletin Inserts* are national church agencies, organizations, programs, projects, campaigns, emphases. Local church leadership determines, filters, selects the *Bulletin Inserts* they want; it has always been obvious that producing an *Insert* does not assure its use in the local congregation!

It is suggested that the local church can produce its own *Bulletin Inserts,* designing them to speak to the interests and priorities of the local community. Since the myriad of *Inserts* cannot all be equally of interest and effectiveness for every parish, why not produce your own?

Congregational leaders can develop *Bulletin Inserts* to address the specific mission interests and concerns which their congregation desires or needs. The *Inserts* can be elementary: first-words or openers on the subject—or, the *Inserts* can be advanced: moving the readers more deeply into an area.

Possible topics for do-it-for-us *Bulletin Inserts* are:

* Information on a church or institution related to congregational interest.
* News items about persons, places, activities.
* Up-to-date data on churchs or mission work.
* Visuals to enhance knowledge and interest: maps, pictures, symbols, graphs, statistics.
* Guidance on action, advocacy, decisions.

The information, stories, news for a *Bulletin Insert* can come from almost anywhere. Some obvious sources are:

* Excerpt from a mission magazine.
* News items from a magazine, newspaper, etc.
* Paragraphs from missionary letters.
* Pictures, maps, visuals from books, magazines, newspapers.

Use the low-cost, readily-available equipment and material already in operation within your parish (or community). Several methods are used to make "electronic stencils," whereby copy (including photos and artwork) can be easily reproduced.

Vary the size of your *Bulletin Insert:* a standard 5 1/2″ × 8 1/2″ sheet, the newly emerging 4 2/3″ × 8 1/2″ (three-folded 14″ legal size paper), a deliberately "oversize" sheet to catch attention.

Color will gain attention—and thus, hopefully, readership. Use colored paper. Try colored ink. If the quantity is not too great, hand color a section.

Artwork aids in making a page or sheet more attractive—and

readable. Collect reproducable pictures, symbols, logos, designs, lettering to enhance your *Insert*.

"White space"—or blank, empty areas—can make your layout much more attractive. Try different type size and/or face. Change the width of columns. Insert "sub-headings." Underline key words, ideas, names.

The simple and ever-present *Bulletin Insert* is an interpretation tool to be created and used by a congregation. Making your own *Inserts* will customize your message, help gain quicker and more responsive readership. Messages and emphases developed specifically for your parish will be welcomed—they will help convey the idea that mission is a part of your life, and not "over there"!

FLAG DISPLAY

Use flag sets and maps in mission interpretation efforts. Arrange flags around a large world or U.S./Canada map (maps from your denomination are possibilities—or one from the National Geographic Society) and identify the various locations around the world, the U.S. and Canada where missionaries are located.

Use flags as a focal point around a table and posters that show partnership in spreading the gospel of Jesus Christ through the U.S./Canada and the world. With string or ribbon from each flag, attach an end to the place of the country or state/province on the map.

Display flags in a suitable location that allows for display of articles, of clothing, books, Bibles, artifacts, pictures, etc. from around the world, labeling each with a country, particularly those represented by the flags. Use a map that will help those looking at the display to locate the various countries or states/provinces.

Small flags available for table or bulletin board displays can be readily available and useful to congregational use. The following sources of such flags can be explored.

1. Wright Studio (source of mission education accessories) located at 56-38 East Washington Street, Indianapolis, Indiana 46219, has a set of 50 stick-pin flags, $2'' \times 5/16''$ printed on heavy paper. The set costs $5.00; add $2.00 for postage and handling. (Payment should accompany order.)
2. The United Nations Association of the United States of

America is located at 300 East 42nd Street, New York, New York 10017. They have available a "UN Flag Chart" which is a large poster of flags of UN member nations. It costs $3.00. They also have a "UN Flag Kit" consisting of miniature paper flags 2 1/2″ × 1″—the kit includes poles, a base and a UN brochure. It costs $7.95. The association will bill postage over 50 cents.

3. The United Nations' Souvenir Shop is located at the UN headquarters, New York, New York 10017. They have UN member country flags in silk 4″ × 6″ at $1.25 each (designate countries desired). Single-hole stands for one flag sell for 40 cents; double-hole stands for two flags sell for 45 cents each. Minimum shipping charge is $2.00. Payment by check or money order is to "United Nations' Souvenir Shop."

4. Annin and Company is one of the largest flag manufacturers and an important source of such resources. Offices are in Verona, New Jersey, 07044, (201-239-9000); Canadian subsidiary: Annin Flag Co., Ltd., 15 Brandon Ave., Toronto, Ont. (416-534-8844). Request their General Trade Catalog which lists US/Canada, foreign, state/province, miniature, religious flags with poles and bases.

MAPS FOR MISSION

A map and mission. These two like faith and works, make sense together.

Think about it. Without a map, it's really hard to do mission— at least the organizational kind. Whether you're part of a congregation looking around at its neighborhood or a churchwide board surveying the world scene, you need to know where the gospel's now at and where you'd like to spread it.

Nor is it easy to appreciate mission without a map. Take the church's first great mission festival described in Acts 2. To really sense its significance, you've got to put a map into it.

Consider the situation: the day was Pentecost, a major harvest festival which the Jews celebrated 50 days after every Passover. So when the apostles got up to speak their Spirit-filled words, they addressed a crowd of pilgrims gathered, as Luke puts it, from "every country in the world."

Many had come from nearby Judea. But others had come from places over a thousand miles away. Rome, the imperial capital, had a delegation, as did Crete, Libya and Egypt. So did Asia, Pontus, Cappadocia, Phrygia and Pamphylia—all provinces in Asia Minor. Likewise Arabia to the south and Parthia, Media, Elam and Mesopotamia to the east.

Truly a polyglot congregation, some of whom the apostles—and the Spirit—that day persuaded to believe and be baptized. Christians returned home, carrying with them the message that Jesus was the Messiah indeed! And so the mission moved into new lands, each a distinct place on the map.

The point is: A map can help Christian mission come alive. It can show where mission has happened, where it is happening, and where it could be happening. It can show not only where the world's four billion-plus people live but also how they have organized themselves politically, what access they have to basic resources, and what their tomorrows might be like.

In short, a map can have meaning beyond itself, especially when made part of mission education efforts. Fortunately for those interested in using them, there's no shortage of useful maps, whether for individual or group study.

A Map That Startles

When you first see the *World Map: Peter's Projection* expect to be startled. For this map, which comes out of Germany, clearly shows that things are not always what they seem.

The style of world map most of us probably cut our geographical teeth on is Mercator's projection, first done in 1569. Though modified periodically during the past four centuries, the map remains the one most widely seen today.

From the beginning, Mercator's map proved a blessing to sailors navigating the world's seas. Unfortunately, however, for the map watcher, it gives some false impressions about relative country sizes. It uses two-thirds of its surface to represent the world's northern half, leaving only a third for the southern half. As a result, the map distorts the earth in favor of the countries inhabited by white people.

In sharp distinction, the Peter's Map, rendered in 1974 by Dr. Arno Peters of Bremen, West Germany, emphasizes land areas and presents the surface of the world more realistically. The result is a world view in which Europe no longer dominates human affairs and in which different areas are brought into true perspective.

This map, to quote from its accompanying text, "is of interest to everyone who cares about mission and wants to understand its place in the world today. In this map the countries of the Third World appear in their correct proportions: North and South come into their own right.

"The map has revealed something yet to be realized in relationships between peoples and nations: a mature partnership of churches and Christians around the world through mutual giving and receiving.

Peter's Map can be a mission education tool by itself—it will start any group talking, asking, reflecting. The map should adorn a wall in every local church, be used in displays and be the map for educational functions. The *World Map: Peter's Projection* is published in the U.S./Canada by Friendship Press—it is available from your denominational bookstore or Friendship Press Distribution Office, P.O. Box 37844, Cincinnati, OH 45222-0844 at a retail price of $7.95.

More Mapping

Investigate other maps to find those useful for your educational purposes. Friendship Press offers a series of *Map 'n' Facts* related to area studies. National Geographic Maps are a good contact (National Geographic Society, 17th & M. Streets, Washington, D.C. 20036). Book stores frequently have a travel section including maps. Large cities have specialty stores offering a wide variety of maps. Check the public library or local colleges/universities for their resources (many geography and history departments have collections which might be borrowed).

Atlas Books published by Hammond, McNally, National Geographic Society and others provide a source for small group examination. An excellent book of maps, well worth the study for global perspective, is *The State of the World Atlas* by Michael Kidron and Ronald Segal; it is published in the United States by Simon and Schuster.

A LITANY OF COMMITMENT TO MISSION

Leader: In confessing Christ today we celebrate God's stead-
fast love, present and powerful in Jesus Christ, by Whose
Spirit the community of faith is gathered.

Response: In confessing Christ today we celebrate the diverse
ways in which the Gospel is proclaimed and the variety of
faithful responses.

Leader: We celebrate our growing awareness that Christians
must stand firm against all injustice, poverty and the systems
and ideologies that enslave body and spirit.

Response: We celebrate the common tasks of service and evangelism to which all disciples of Christ are called.

Leader: To love the world which God so loved that Christ
emptied Himself for its salvation:

Response: We commit ourselves, O Lord.

Leader: We commit ourselves to care for nature and to work
for the spiritual and physical welfare of all people

Response: We commit ourselves to greater acceptance of the
Gospel's bias toward the poor and mistreated and pledge to
labor more diligently for the liberation of those who are
oppressed by poverty, social injustice and political tyranny,
and for the deliverance as well of those who are the op-
pressors.

Leader: To a deepening understanding that mission is not measured by apparent success but by faithfulness to Christ:

Response: We commit ourselves, O Lord.

Leader: As Christians we stand firm in the belief that God will
eventually vindicate the promises and assurances of the Gospel.

Response: We accept the continuing pilgrimage, no matter
how long and confusing it may be, for we know he comes
to greet us.

AMEN.

(Adapted from the statement *Pilgrimage in Mission: Learnings Along the Way*, United
Methodist Church, General Board of Global Ministries.)

IX. ON USING THIS BOOK

by John S. Kerr

This book provides a many-faceted resource for both understanding mission more deeply and enriching one's own mission. The brief readings in the first half stimulate reflection. The many suggestions in the last half will open eyes to new possibilities for mission education and outreach.

PERSONAL STUDY

Being in Mission lends itself to personal study by persons who have an interest in widening their concept of mission. For example reading sections I, II, and III would require about a month, taking one reading each day. Readers might consider this as their daily devotional exercise, and may agree to reflect on each reading in a prayerful way, jotting down brief notes on their thoughts and reflections.

At the end of the month readers might come together to share insights, feelings, and fresh visions of mission. Afterward this group might form a nucleus to promote mission education throughout the congregation. For this stage, sections VII and VIII provide important suggestions and ideas.

Even without the group commitment of this approach, the book can be used for enriching individuals. The book could be put into the hands of people who would profit from a deeper grasp of mission. Make a personal visit, if possible. Point out specific readings which may interest each individual. One might focus this effort on key leaders who have responsibility for the mission of the congregation.

Wider audiences of concerned persons in the pews can be reached by displaying copies of this book in the narthex of the church or in the church library. Announce its availability. Station someone near the display to help prospective readers. It is important to point out that this book consists of brief readings which require only a couple of minutes each.

GROUP STUDY

Any organized study group will profit from this book. It may be a new study group formed especially to explore this book as a way to get deeper into mission.

With its accent on doing and enriching mission, this book makes an excellent study for leadership groups, such as committees and church council. This study works especially well with these groups if it leads toward planning for mission. Planning includes understanding the dynamics and theology of mission, evaluating the congregational program in light of a deeper grasp of mission, and planning new ventures in both mission and mission education. *Being in Mission* provides convenient resources for each of these steps.

The church council or an appropriate committee could, for example, spend 30 minutes or so of each meeting over a period of time on a planning process for mission. Some congregations might want to appoint a special committee for this purpose.

The following is an outline of four brief study and planning sessions. The process leads to setting in motion new ventures in mission and mission education.

Session One: *Understanding Mission*

Start by writing the word *mission* on the chalkboard or newsprint. Ask participants to suggest words or phrases which they feel explain the term *mission*. Write their contributions around the word *mission* on the chalkboard or newsprint. (Save this.)

Read and discuss "The Church in Mission," using the questions provided. Form sub-groups of two or three participants to identify the marks of mission which appear most clearly in the life of the congregation, and those which need cultivation. Share these comments in the whole group. Keep a positive tone. You are doing mission now, but you want to do more. Identify specific activities which represent the marks of mission you now display. Then look at the marks which need enrichment. What specific activities might enhance these areas? List all these activities in a way which lets you save them for future sessions.

Move on to "Stewards of Mission." You can talk about stories of people in your congregation who are doing mission. Or sub-groups can write stories and share them with the whole group.

Then ask, "What kinds of stories could we tell if we had the sort of mission here that we dream of?" This gets the group thinking about new possibilities in a story form that lends reality to their vision. Simply saying, "We need a better evangelism program" doesn't carry the punch of an idealized story about someone witnessing at work. Such stories, by putting flesh on abstractions, point directions for future programs. In this case, it may suggest more need to train people in personal witnessing than to develop a more extensive calling program.

In closing, invite participants to read the other selections in sections I and II at home. Offer a prayer.

Session Two: *Looking At Our Mission*

At the start of the session, ask participants to share insights from their own reading in *Being In Mission*.

Form into four sub-groups. (In a small group, a sub-group may have one person. But at least two work better. You can combine assignments to use two sub-groups, if necessary.) Assign each sub-group a different reading: "The Open Secret," "Sent Free," "Evangelism—The Heart of the Mission Task," and "Mission and Justice." Ask each sub-group to read their item and discuss it, using the questions for guidelines. When finished, each sub-group will report a summary of their reading and discussion to the whole group.

Bring out the definitions of mission from Session One. Any new insights, new words, or changes in what they said earlier?

Ask, "What did we learn about our own mission?" "What have we seen as strong mission in our congregation?" "What clues have we gained for deepening our mission?"

As suggestions come forth, list them along with suggestions from the previous session. You might make a double-column list: "Affirmations" and "Future Hopes." The "Affirmation" list includes activities you now do which participants perceive as healthy expressions of mission. The "Future Hopes" list collects ideas for new activities or ways to enrich present activities. The lists will reveal something of the variety of mission.

If your group seems to identify mission largely with traditional church-type activities—such as evangelism, worship, and such—

read and discuss "On Being Stewards" to gain a different perspective. Concepts in that reading may help the group perceive
concern for environment, fellowship endeavors, community service and similar activities as authentic expressions of mission.

Save all the lists. Invite participants to read further on their
own in section III. Close with sentence prayers for mission.

Session Three: *Helping Us All Toward Mission*

This session focuses on mission education, deepening the mission
consciousness of all members. The ways you have already identified for enhancing mission will require motivated people. Mission education provides a vehicle for the Spirit of God, who
ultimately is the real motivator for mission.

Divide into sub-groups of two persons. Ask each pair to do
the evaluation under "Stop: Evaluate." Remind them to consider
mission in its broadest sense, including both the local mission
of the congregation and the congregation's involvement in national and international mission. Each pair will report their eval-
uations to the whole group. You can make an "average" rating
for each item on a master list. Maintain a positive mood. The
group is building a better future mission, and not just criticizing
the present.

Then ask the group to read and discuss "Building Excitement
About Mission." That segment lists some common activities in
every congregation, along with ways you can give them a stronger
mission focus. Comparing those activities with the items on the
"Stop: Evaluate" listing, ask the group to identify *specific* activities the congregation could include in its preaching, teaching,
worship, fellowship and service dimensions which would enhance mission education and motivation. Add these suggestions
to your growing list of ideas.

Ask the group to read "Structures for Mission" before the next
session, and invite them to skim through chapters VII and VIII,
checking off activities and programs they think would benefit
the congregation.

Close with prayer.

Session Four: *Moving Into New Mission*

This session concentrates on initiating new mission activities.

Bring to the session all the lists of ideas for new activities and
ventures in mission that have been developed in previous ses-

sions. If the lists look a bit rough, recopy them on newsprint, using big letters so all can read them.

Start off by reading and discussing "Planning," in order to get a perspective on the planning process. Developing a mission statement for the congregation is an important step toward planning for and implementing effective mission. A cross-section of the congregation should become involved in this process, and the process in itself is a powerful mission education tool. The group may wish to initiate such a process.

From their readings of chapters VII and VIII, collect ideas which struck individuals as worthwhile. Add them to your lists.

Next, evaluate all the ideas the group has generated. Ask them for priorities. Which are "musts"? Which can wait? When you determine your "must" priorities, review them again. Is the list too ambitious? Does it include some really fresh and exciting ideas?

When you approve a final "must" list, begin the process of putting these activities into action. Decide which activities fall under existing committees, and which might require a new committee or sub-committee. Ask the group to commit themselves to seeing these proposals through the structures of the congregation. Create a timeline for each new proposal, assigning a person responsibility for each step of its implementation. Set a time, perhaps two or three months ahead, when you will meet again to evaluate progress.

Close with prayer, and with thanks to the group for their good efforts.